YORK NOTES

ATONEMENT

IAN MCEWAN

Notes by Anne Rooney
Revised by Lyn Lockwood

PEARSON

YORK
PRESS

YORK PRESS
322 Old Brompton Road, London SW5 9JH

PEARSON EDUCATION LIMITED
Edinburgh Gate, Harlow,
Essex CM20 2JE, United Kingdom

Associated companies, branches and representatives throughout the world

First published 2006
This new and fully revised edition 2016

10 9 8 7 6 5 4 3 2

ISBN: 978–1–2921–3816–9

Illustration on page 57 by Alan Batley
Phototypeset by Carnegie Book Production
Printed in Slovakia

Photo credits: Tischenko Irina/Shutterstock for page 6 / Ragne Kabanova/Shutterstock for page 7 / tviolet/Shutterstock for page 8 / Alex James Bramwell/Shutterstock for page 9 / © Purestock/Alamy Stock Photo/Alamy for page 10 / Rocksweeper/Shutterstock for page 12 / elblanc/Thinkstock for page 13 top / purplequeue/Shutterstock for page 13 bottom / Rusty Pelican/Shutterstock for page 14 / ads861/Shutterstock for page 15 top / Thomas-bethge/Thinkstock for page 15 bottom / Matusciac/Shutterstock for page 16 / Pamela D.Maxwell/Shutterstock for page 18 / Nejron Photo/ Shutterstock for page 19 middle / Mary Rice/Shutterstock for page 19 bottom / © Fritz Photography Teens/Alamy Stock Photo/Alamy for page 20 / Burlingham/Shutterstock for page 21 / LianeM/Shutterstock for page 22 / Stefano Cavoretto/Shutterstock for page 23 / Yanas/Shutterstock for page 24 / © M.Flynn/Alamy Stock Photo/Alamy for page 25 / LydiaGoolia/Thinkstock for page 26 / Napatsan Puakpong/Shutterstock for page 27 / gnagel/ Thinkstock for page 29 / PlusONE/Shutterstock for page 30 / © Fritz Photography Teens/Alamy Stock Photo/Alamy for page 31/ Vlue/Shutterstock for page 32 top / Pascal Halder/Shutterstock for page 32 bottom / Lina_Aster/Shutterstock for page 33 / Berents/Shutterstock for page 34 / Sandra Cunningham/Shutterstock for page 35 / Wanchai Orsuk/Shutterstock for page 36 / melis/Shutterstock for page 37 / johnbraid/Shutterstock for page 38 / Voyagerix/Shutterstock for page 39 / pedrosala/Shutterstock for page 41 / Gary Blakeley/Shutterstock for page 42 / Poly Liss/Shutterstock for page 43 / Pedro Monteiro/Shutterstock for page 44 / Brooke Becker/Shutterstock for page 45 / Ti Santi/Shutterstock for page 46 / Oleg Golovnev/ Shutterstock for page 47 top / spinetta/Shutterstock for page 47 bottom / Christopher Lyzcen/Shutterstock for page 48 top / George C. Beresford/ Stringer/Getty for page 48 bottom / Matt Ragen/Shutterstock for page 49 / Skyearth/Shutterstock for page 50 / Seregam/Shutterstock for page 51 / Mike Mols/Shutterstock for page 52 / Neamov/Shutterstock for page 53 / Eric Isselee/Shutterstock for page 54 top / 1000 words/Shutterstock for page 54 middle / Alexander Mazurkevich/Shutterstock for page 56 / Kris butler/Thinkstock for page 58 / lukas_zb/Thinkstock for page 60 / solominviktor/Shutterstock for page 62 / © Fritz Photography Teens/Alamy Stock Photo/Alamy for page 64 / azndc/Thinkstock for page 65 / Nejron Photo/Shutterstock for page 66 / Steve Allen/Shutterstock for page 67 / Burlingham/Shutterstock for page 68 top / Alice Day/Shutterstock for page 68 bottom / Arena Creative/Shutterstock for page 69 / rothivan/Thinkstock for page 70 top / YSK1/Shutterstock for page 70 bottom / Sergey Kamshylin/Shutterstock for page 71 top / Manfred Ruckszio/Shutterstock for page 71 bottom / f9photos/Shutterstock for page 73 / taviphoto/ Shutterstock for page 74 / trekandshoot/Shutterstock for page 75 / Brovkina/Shutterstock for page 76 / Judy Kennamer/Shutterstock for page 77 / Tais Policanti/Shutterstock for page 78 /AMC Photography/Shutterstock for page 79 / LanKS/Shutterstock for page 82 / Ysbrand Cosijn/Shutterstock for page 83 / Arina P Habich/Shutterstock for page 84 / akiyoko/Shutterstock for page 85 / margo_black/Shutterstock for page 86 / Arno van Dulmen/Shutterstock for page 87 / D and S Photographic Services / Shutterstock for page 88 / March of Time/Getty for page 90 / Misunseo/ Shutterstock for page 91 / Svetlana Kuznetsova/Shutterstock for page 92 / Triff/Shutterstock for page 93 / Marco Secchi/Getty for page 94 / Butterfly Hunter/Shutterstock for page 95 / Everett Historical/Shutterstock for page 97 / Carl Mydans/Getty Images for page 98

PART FIVE: CONTEXTS AND INTERPRETATIONS

PART SIX: PROGRESS BOOSTER

PART SEVEN: FURTHER STUDY AND ANSWERS

HOW TO USE YOUR YORK NOTES TO STUDY AND REVISE *ATONEMENT*

These Notes can be used in a range of ways to help you read, study and revise for your exam or assessment.

Become an informed and independent reader

Throughout the Notes, you will find the following key features to aid your study:

- **'Key context'** margin features: these widen your knowledge of the setting, whether historical, social or political. This is highlighted by the AO3 (Assessment Objective 3) symbol to remind you of its connection to aspects you may want to refer to in your exam responses.

- **'Key interpretation'** boxes (a key part of AO5 on AQA – AO5 is not assessed by Edexcel in relation to *Atonement*): do you agree with the perspective or idea that is explained here? Does it help you form your own view on events or characters? Developing your own interpretations is a key element of higher-level achievement in A Level, so make use of this and similar features.

- **'Key connection'** features (linked to AO4): whether or not you refer to such connections in your exam writing, having a wider understanding of how the novel, or aspects of it, links to other texts or ideas can give you new perspectives on the text.

- **'Study focus'** panels: these help to secure your own understanding of key elements of the text. Being able to write in depth on a particular point or explain a specific feature will help your writing sound professional and informed.

- **'Key quotation'** features: these identify the effect of specific language choices – you could use these for revision purposes at a later date.

- **'Progress booster'** features: these offer specific advice about how to tackle a particular aspect of your study, or an idea you might want to consider discussing in your exam responses.

- **'Extract analysis'** sections: these are vital for you to use either during your reading or when you come back to the text afterwards. These sections take a core extract from a chapter and explore it in real depth, explaining its significance and impact, raising questions and offering interpretations.

Stay on track with your study and revision

Your first port of call will always be your teacher, and you should already have a good sense of how well you are doing, but the Notes offer you several ways of measuring your progress.

- **'Revision task'**: throughout the Notes, there are some challenging, but achievable, written tasks for you to do relevant to the section just covered. Suggested answers are supplied in **Part Seven**.

- **'Progress check'**: this feature comes at the end of **Parts Two** to **Five**, and contains a range of short and longer tasks which address key aspects of the Part of the Notes you have just read. Below this is a grid of key skills which you can complete to track your progress, and rate your understanding.

- **'Practice task'** and **'Mark scheme'**: use these features to make a judgement on how well you know the text and how well you can apply the skills you have learnt.

Most importantly, enjoy using these Notes and see your knowledge and skills improve.

The edition used in these Notes is the Vintage Future Classics edition, 2002.

 **PROGRESS BOOSTER**

You can choose to use the Notes as you wish, but as you read the novel it can be useful to read over the **Part Two** summaries and analysis in order to embed key events, ideas and developments in the **narrative**.

A02 **PROGRESS BOOSTER**

Don't forget to make full use of **Parts Three** to **Five** of the Notes during your reading of the novel. You may have essays to complete on genre, or key themes, or on the impact of specific settings, and can therefore make use of these in-depth sections. Or you may simply want to check out a particular idea or area as you're reading or studying the novel in class.

A01 **PROGRESS BOOSTER**

Part Six: Progress booster will introduce you to different styles of question and how to tackle them; help you to improve your expression so that it has a suitably academic and professional tone; assist you with planning and use of evidence to support ideas; and, most importantly, show you three sample exam responses at different levels with helpful AO-related annotations and follow-up comments. Dedicating time to working through this Part will be something you won't regret.

ATONEMENT: A SNAPSHOT

A modern classic?

Atonement was published in 2001 and seemed to achieve 'classic' status almost immediately. It was an instant bestseller around the world, it won many awards, was quickly regarded as a text worthy not just of turning into a film (2007, directed by Joe Wright) but also of academic study at A Level and beyond. The story spans the twentieth century and, although it can be challenging to read, it is often described as an absorbing family drama, love story and historical saga. So why is *Atonement* so enjoyed and so widely studied in the twenty-first century?

Atonement as a historical novel

Excepting the modern-day **epilogue** to the novel, *Atonement* is set during, and just before, the Second World War, its action taking place in 1935 and 1940. Many **historical novels** can be described as **popular fiction**, in which the setting may aid the creation of an escapist fantasy world. *Atonement* does not use its historical setting in this way. Instead, the time in which it is set is vital to the unfolding of the action.

Literature that endures and remains enjoyable and relevant over years or even centuries always contains an account of experience that is common to people from different cultures. It examines themes such as death, love, loss, personal development and ambition, all of which are unchanging parts of the human condition. Historical fiction relies on these unchanging features of being human for its power. It reassures us that people have always been the same, helps us to **identify** with others in different cultural contexts and endorses our own experiences. But it must also be rooted in the period in which it is set, observing the different social conditions and customs of the time and showing how they affect people and events. In *Atonement*, it is the impact of these social conditions and customs, and of the very particular event of the Second World War, that determines the outcome. The feelings, actions, hopes and fears of the characters could be the same in any time and place, but the circumstances in which they are set largely determine what happens.

What is 'atonement'?

The concept of 'atonement' refers to making up for one's sins. It is a crucial idea in Roman Catholicism, references to which surface intermittently in the novel. It also involves coming to terms with one's own altered state and accepting what has happened – 'at-one-ment'. This is clearly the **narrator** Briony's problematic journey in the book but other characters also look for ways of dealing with their 'sins' and mistakes, such as silent victim Lola Quincey and neglectful mother Emily Tallis.

The puzzle of *Atonement*

Atonement is a **reflexive novel**, in that it is a book about how the book itself came to be written – almost a 'book within a book'. Even though novels which reflect on the process of their own writing, such as J. D. Salinger's *The Catcher in the Rye* (1951), are not unusual, they present particular challenges for the reader. The elderly Briony, too, comments on how she has drafted and redrafted the story, saying 'there's always a certain kind of reader who will be compelled to ask, But what *really* happened?' (p. 371). As McEwan examines the process of writing, so we need to examine the process of our own reading and our relationship to the narrator and the novelist.

A book about books

As we would expect in a novel which looks directly at the process of its own composition, there is a great deal in *Atonement* about writing, imagination, memory, the past, the nature of the truth and the role of literature. There are frequent references and **allusions** to other works and writers. It is not necessary to recognise all of these, though a knowledge of some will enrich your reading of *Atonement*.

A challenging text

Atonement is challenging, too, in its deeply distressing depictions of the violence and horrors of battle. McEwan makes no attempt to hide the terrors of war, but presents an unrelenting stream of images of injury and distress that leave us reeling. However, the violence and sexual perversion which seemed gratuitous to some reviewers of McEwan's earlier fiction are maturely realised and fully embedded in *Atonement*. Paul Marshall – a 'maniac', to borrow Lola's term – is all the more alarming for his apparent normality. The image of Lola and Paul Marshall marrying – the rapist marrying his victim – is particularly shocking. We could argue that McEwan uses such horror to explore moral questions and values rather than just for its own effect.

Briony Tallis: The unreliable narrator

Briony does not reveal herself as the ultimate narrator until the very end of the book. This forces us into a re-evaluation of all we have read and thought up to this point because we appear to have heard several voices describing events from their own points of view. As Briony has proved to be an unreliable witness, and finally to be suffering the early stages of dementia, we are left with a very fluid idea of what happened, how it happened and what, if anything, it all means.

A02

Study focus: Key issues to explore

As you study the text and revise for the exam, keep in mind these key elements and ideas:

- The unreliable nature of Briony as the narrator of the story
- The effects of war on human behaviour
- The nature of forgiveness
- How we achieve 'atonement' for our mistakes
- The power of money and social class
- The process of writing and telling stories
- The relationship between the present and the past
- Our ability to separate fact and fiction
- The enduring nature of Robbie and Cecilia's love

In each case, make sure you develop your own interpretations and, with the help of these Notes, prepare to argue your viewpoint on them.

A04 KEY CONNECTION

In all McEwan's fiction there is a key moment, often an accidental event, which leads to the destruction of a life or of lives. In *The Child in Time* (1987), for example, a man looks away from his young daughter in a supermarket and loses her forever. In *Atonement*, Briony's catastrophic misinterpretation of Robbie and Cecilia's behaviour plays a similar role.

A03 KEY CONTEXT

McEwan has demonstrated a keen interest in politics and the morality of the political regimes of the late twentieth century. He has spoken against nuclear arms and on the terrorist attacks on New York (2001) and London (2005). The next novel after *Atonement*, *Saturday* (2005), set on the brink of the Iraq war (2003–4), reflects on personal responses and responsibility for violence.

SYNOPSIS

Melodrama and misunderstandings

Atonement is divided into three parts and an **epilogue**. The first part, taking up half of the book, is set on the hottest day of 1935 on the English country estate of the Tallis family, and revolves around a family get-together. The Tallises' upper-class life is depicted at length in a slow-moving portrait of the day, seemingly from different points of view. Thirteen-year-old Briony Tallis is trying to produce a **melodrama** she has written, with parts performed by her three visiting cousins. She gives up on this, after witnessing through a window an unusual incident: her older sister Cecilia strips off her clothes and plunges into the fountain in the grounds of their house, watched by Robbie (the son of the cleaning lady), who is treated as a member of the Tallis family. Unaware that Cecilia is retrieving a valuable vase she and Robbie have just broken, Briony does not understand what she sees and assumes that Robbie has forced her into this act in some way.

A note delivered

Robbie, realising he is attracted to Cecilia, writes her a note, then adds an obscene ending. He rewrites it, but accidentally gives Briony the obscene note to carry ahead to Cecilia. Briony opens it and reads it, and is horrified at what she finds. She passes the note to Cecilia, who realises her sister has read it. On the way from her room to dinner, Briony happens to go into the library, where Cecilia and Robbie are making love. Misinterpreting again, she assumes Robbie was attacking her sister and is a dangerous madman. After an awkward dinner, two of her cousins, twin boys, go out of the room, leaving a note to say they have run away. The party breaks up to search for them.

A witness to a terrible crime

Briony goes to the island in the lake, where she finds her other cousin, Lola, with a man just leaving her. It appears that Lola has been attacked, and Briony quickly convinces herself that Robbie is the rapist. When Robbie returns from the hunt for the twins, having found both of them, he is arrested. The police question all the family at length and Briony repeatedly states that Robbie was the man she saw with Lola. He is eventually imprisoned for the rape.

KEY CONNECTION A04

At the start of *Atonement*, Ian McEwan includes a quote from Jane Austen's (1775–1817) novel *Northanger Abbey*. The heroine, Catherine Morland, is an avid reader of Gothic novels, and, like Briony, has difficulty in observing the boundaries between reality and fiction. She comes to believe that the inhabitants of Northanger Abbey hide a dreadful secret and that terrible deeds have been committed there. In the quotation, Catherine is reprimanded for allowing her imagination to run wild in this way. McEwan has sometimes referred to *Atonement* as his 'Jane Austen novel'.

PROGRESS BOOSTER A01

Ensure you are aware of who appears to be telling the story as *Atonement* has different **narrative** layers. Sometimes we appear to hear events from the point of view of a different character, such as Emily Tallis, but the account is all ultimately written by Briony Tallis and as such is possibly biased and unreliable.

The war in France

The second part of the novel is set five years later in northern France during the retreat of the British army to Dunkirk. Robbie and two corporals, Nettle and Mace, are making their way to the beach for the evacuation. Robbie has served part of his prison sentence for rape. They travel through the French countryside, witnessing the horrors of war and being caught in repeated German air attacks. It starts to become clear that Robbie's undressed wounds are infected; this becomes progressively worse during the walk to Dunkirk, making him delirious and prone to hallucinations. This part of the novel ends with Robbie sleeping in the cellar of a house in Dunkirk the night before the evacuation from the beaches. During this section we also learn that Robbie and Cecilia are still in love, but have maintained their relationship only by letter. Cecilia no longer sees her family because they would not accept Robbie's innocence. Briony has at last offered to retract her original statement and admit publicly that Robbie is innocent.

A nurse in London

The third part of the novel also takes place in the summer of 1940 and is set in England. Briony has become a trainee nurse and is working in a London hospital. Within a few days, the hospital is transformed when the wounded from Dunkirk begin to arrive on the wards. Briony quickly learns the skills she needs to deal with their terrible injuries and to handle the trauma of caring for them. Still determined to be a writer, Briony has written a story based on what she saw at the fountain as a child, but it is rejected by a magazine.

A wedding

Briony learns that Paul Marshall and Lola are to marry. She goes to the church, uninvited, to watch the small wedding. After the service, she goes to Cecilia's flat. Their meeting is very tense. Cecilia remains hostile and resentful towards Briony. Robbie, who is also in the flat, finds it hard to control his fury. Cecilia and Robbie are both surprised to learn from Briony that she is now certain that Paul committed the rape. They are also angered to hear of Paul and Lola's marriage, as it will not now be possible to bring Paul to justice. At the end of the meeting, Robbie makes Briony promise to swear a legal oath, to tell her parents the truth and to write a full account of what really happened. This account will become *Atonement*.

Briony's final years

In an epilogue written by Briony in 1999, we learn that the novel is the culmination of a series of drafts she has created during her life – her act of atonement. Briony sees Paul and Lola, now Lord and Lady Marshall, from a distance when she visits the Imperial War Museum. She acknowledges that her book cannot be published until Paul and Lola are dead, which will probably be after her own death, as she has had a diagnosis of dementia. She attends a party for her birthday held in the old Tallis family home, now a country-house hotel, where her melodrama is finally performed. Briony explains that this current version of *Atonement* (and the one we are reading) portrays Cecilia and Robbie alive and together at the end. In all previous versions she followed the true pattern of events, in which, she suggests, they both die before 1940.

PART ONE, CHAPTER ONE

Summary

- Briony Tallis, the youngest daughter of a civil-servant father and a semi-invalid mother, has written a play – a **melodrama** – which she intends to perform with her cousins for her older brother Leon on his return home to their country estate.
- The family lives in a large house in the English countryside with servants and land. It is a very hot day in the summer of 1935.
- Briony has a passion for writing and considers herself to have talent and promise. She experiments with new words she reads in a dictionary and **thesaurus**, and examples of her inexpert use of these are given, inviting us to laugh gently at her.
- Her cousins, fifteen-year-old Lola and twins Pierrot and Jackson, are refugees from a broken home who will be staying in the Tallis household while their mother is in Paris with a new lover.
- The rehearsals for the play quickly disappoint and frustrate Briony as Lola takes the lead role, which Briony had written for herself, and the boys prove at first reluctant and then inept.

Analysis

Briony's point of view

Although events are related by an anonymous, third-person **narrator**, the voice in many passages is that of Briony. She is the central character of the early part of the book and the one who will seek the 'atonement' of the title. Only at the very end of the book do we discover that the whole story is being told by the older Briony.

We see hints of Briony's literary ambition immediately in phrases such as 'a two-day tempest of composition' and 'the distant north' (p. 3), the latter a **cliché** from the type of children's books she would have spent hours reading. The style which characterises the passages presented from Briony's point of view is self-regarding, ostentatiously 'literary' and often flamboyant. By the end of the first page, the full, extravagant extent of her literary pretensions has been laid bare in the outline of the melodrama she has written, *The Trials of Arabella*. Her active imagination is demonstrated again as she fantasises about the effect the play will have on her brother – as far as guiding him to choose a suitable bride who would make Briony her bridesmaid.

Study focus: McEwan's intervention

A02

Notice how McEwan tells us that the performance will not in fact take place. In slipping out of Briony's young voice and telling us in advance that the play will not reach fulfilment, McEwan breaks the chronological flow of the **narrative** and frustrates our natural keenness to see what will happen. At many key points in the novel, and several minor ones like this, we are told how things will turn out. This undermines **dramatic tension** but has the effect of forcing us to focus on how events and characters affect one another. As we already know what will happen, we turn our attention to how it will happen. How events lead to one another and why events turn out as they do are major concerns of the book.

Progress booster: Character development

Briony's character is developed considerably as we hear about her writing, her liking for order and her desire for secrets. Her personality is conveyed as much in the use of language, which copies Briony's own vocabulary, as in the relation of, and commentary on, events. Make sure that you can comment on the vocabulary McEwan uses to develop Briony's character in this chapter, and his use of the same technique elsewhere in the novel.

A tragedy within a tragedy?

Briony's melodrama, we are told, was intended to 'inspire ... terror, relief and instruction, in that order' (p. 8). This is an **allusion** to Aristotle's *Poetics*, a critical text on writing drama composed in Athens during the fourth century BC. Aristotle says that the nature of tragedy is to inspire terror and pity in the safe environment of the theatre and then to relieve them in the drama's **resolution**. The question of whether literature has a duty of instruction also has a long history.

A slow start

The opening chapter is used largely to introduce Briony and her literary ambitions, though the action gets under way (for us and Briony) once the cousins arrive. It is a slow and languorous start to the novel and sets up the feeling that 'not much happens', which is sustained throughout most of Part One.

Study focus: The narrator

It is important to note how the narrator keeps some emotional distance between herself (and therefore us) and the young Briony. We are given opportunities to laugh at Briony, to enjoy our own superior knowledge of vocabulary, literary forms, and the actions and motivation of adolescent girls. We are told that she has probably never heard of melodrama, but at the same time we are expected to recognise the allusion to scholarly debates about literature.

At one point the narrator lays claim to uncertainty about Briony's inner state – 'Perhaps she herself was struggling with the temptation to flounce from the room' (p. 16). On one level, this is clearly a **conceit** – McEwan knows what he intends Briony's thoughts and feelings to be. But it also acknowledges that once created a story and its characters take on lives of their own, beyond the author's intentions – a fact that escapes the young Briony, who seeks to control every aspect of her creation.

Key quotation: Nothing to hide

One cryptic line offers a suggestion of how later events might be understood. We are told that Briony's lack of opportunity to hide real secrets was not 'particularly an affliction; or rather, it appeared so only in retrospect, once a solution had been found' (p. 5). The secret which comes to dominate and ruin the lives of the central characters is casually signposted here as 'a solution' to the problem of Briony having nothing to hide.

A03 KEY CONTEXT

Tragedy and melodrama are very different. In a tragedy, a hero of epic stature is brought from a high status to death through a reversal of fortune. There is no place for sentiment, random misfortune or motiveless actions. Such a hero's fall is caused by a 'fatal flaw' in their character which means their response to events leads to their downfall. It is important that the hero recognises how their own failings have caused their doom. The action must be consistent and complete, and not depend on anything outside the scope of the tragedy. Both Briony and Robbie could be seen to have some of these characteristics, although neither is a straightforward tragic hero.

A03 KEY CONTEXT

When Briony uses cholera as the illness her heroine is suffering from, she may have been thinking of the respiratory disease consumption (tuberculosis). This is more commonly used as an illness in melodrama and has **Romantic** associations. Victims have pale skin and very rosy cheeks.

EXTRACT ANALYSIS: CHAPTER ONE (PP. 5–6)

The first chapter of the novel introduces Briony's character at thirteen years of age. The way Briony is presented here will affect how we see her and judge her actions. Even though there will be a chance to reappraise this picture in the light of coming events, the first introduction to a character makes a lasting impression. What is revealed about Briony in these pages, therefore, carries considerable weight.

The voice describing Briony appears to be that of an **omniscient narrator** who has privileged insights into her mental state. A sense of Briony's own dissatisfaction with her unexciting life comes through, though. That no one wanted to know about the squirrel's skull sounds like the sulky complaint of a petulant child. This method of presenting a character's own views or realm of consciousness by giving the narrator words or turns of phrase that could be the character's own is used throughout *Atonement*. The language holds a great deal of pent-up energy and potential for disaster. Even though the text is saying that these things are *not* present – 'mayhem', 'destruction', 'chaotic', 'cruel' (p. 5) – we sense them lurking under the surface. It will transpire that Briony's life and character also conceal suppressed imaginative energy, which will be released with catastrophic results.

KEY CONTEXT (A03)

McEwan, like Briony, felt that he grew up as an only child because his stepbrother and stepsister were much older than he was.

Briony's life is shown to be ordered and harmonious. It sounds dull, but as she hates disorder she appears reasonably satisfied with it. She enjoys social advantage, but there is nothing interesting in her life. The following line is ominous: 'None of this was particularly an affliction; or rather, it appeared so only in retrospect, once a solution had been found' (p. 5). It tells us that something will happen but it is cryptic. This comment gives the first hint of **narrative tension** after a slow start. Only much later will it become apparent that the fact that there were no real secrets or intrigues in Briony's life led her to fashion one out of the events and characters around her, with dire consequences.

This passage goes on to introduce the theme of writing which will be central to the book. Although Briony's play has already been mentioned, it has not previously been clear that this is the latest in a series of compositions. The language of this passage suggests the insights of an experienced writer, though it also expresses the thirteen-year-old writer's dissatisfaction with her earlier work. Briony's embarrassment leads her to keep her writing secret until a work is finished, and her anxiety that she is revealing too much of herself will be familiar to anyone who has tried creative writing. Her assumption that people will think she is writing about herself is partly justified. The fact that Briony has had little experience of the world so far is not necessarily a hindrance; for details of human experience, all writers must look inwards, hoping that what they find has general applicability and will be recognised by their readers. Briony's subject matter in the **melodrama** is, however, far outside her own realm of experience. In her early work she can, to a certain extent, start to imagine other people's lives through her writing, but she is a long way from imagining other people's psyches.

A03 **KEY CONTEXT**

A writer's earlier work, called **juvenilia**, can hold clues to how they develop later. In the **epilogue**, Briony says that she has gone full circle, returning to the satisfying moral pattern of *The Trials of Arabella* by reworking the ending of her story to reunite the lovers, Cecilia and Robbie.

There is **irony** in Briony's worry that the reader would speculate about her representing herself because we later discover that this is indeed the older Briony writing about her younger self. There is irony, too, in the assertions that 'she did not have it in her to be cruel' (p. 5) and that her ordered life denied her any possibility of wrongdoing. Although Briony is not wilfully cruel, she turns out to be astonishingly thoughtless and inconsiderate and Robbie, misunderstanding her motives, does believe her cruel and even vindictive. She manages to create chaos and destruction through her urge to make everything neat – the very urge which supposedly prevents her from doing wrong.

Briony's desire for order and harmony expressed in the neatness of her room is mirrored in the pattern of her **narratives**, both her written fiction and her account of what happened on the island. Briony's habit of writing stories in which fates are resolved and 'the whole matter sealed off at both ends' (p. 6) demonstrates the impulse that will soon lead to disaster. It is because she tries to impose a similar balance on the events and characters of real life, moulding them to make a story, that her imagination is able to wreak such havoc on those around her.

PART ONE, CHAPTER TWO

Summary

- Cecilia Tallis, Briony's sister, has picked flowers for the guest room which is being prepared for Paul Marshall.
- She takes a valuable vase with an important family history to fill with water at a fountain in the garden and runs into Robbie, the son of the cleaning lady. Robbie has been educated at the Tallises' expense and both Cecilia and Robbie have been to Cambridge University.
- Relations between the pair are strained. As Cecilia rejects Robbie's offer of help with filling the vase, they break the vase and two fragments fall to the bottom of the fountain.
- Again refusing Robbie's help, Cecilia undresses and retrieves the fragments, then stalks into the house.

Analysis

Cecilia's voice

The narratorial voice has changed for this chapter, and we observe events from Cecilia's point of view, rather than Briony's. Her voice comes through quite clearly, as she describes everything in the scene with a precision and care that make it possible to visualise it exactly, such as the 'wintry sedge' and the 'unused rosewood music stands' (p. 20). She carefully observes not just her surroundings but herself in them. Cecilia describes events and scenery as though she is imagining how her description will be judged, and places herself in the scene with a keen awareness of how she appears to Robbie as well as to readers. Cecilia drily comments that 'There was something between them, and even she had to acknowledge that a tame remark about the weather sounded perverse' (p. 25).

A hot summer's day

The extensive description makes the chapter move slowly. Time is expended on recounting and analysing the smallest details. This contributes to the languid, even sluggish, air of the hot summer day as well as giving a sense of Cecilia's intimate relationship with the Tallis house and gardens. Cecilia tries to break out of this languor herself, by running, by plunging into cold water, by refreshing the flowers – but her slow prose always undermines these attempts.

Later events will make the drama of the broken vase look absurd, and by the end of the book we are told the vase is smashed beyond repair by Betty the cook when the house is being reorganised. Here, however, its importance is easily exaggerated as nothing else is happening. This slightly surreal incident is typical of the unexpected and resonant acts that characters often carry out in Ian McEwan's books.

Study focus: The breaking of the vase

A02

The only event in this chapter is the breaking of the vase. By explaining its history, Cecilia gives the vase something of a mythical status. The build-up makes the accident more dramatic, and Cecilia's carefully calculated response milks it for every last bit of impact. She chooses her own actions to make Robbie feel as bad as possible, revelling in his distress and reiterating that it is his 'punishment' every time she thinks of another way of making him uncomfortable. In her final, ludicrous thought that 'Drowning herself would be his punishment' (p. 30), we glimpse something of her sister Briony's overdramatisation.

Cecilia and Robbie's developing relationship

Although the events of the chapter are slight, there is turmoil beneath the surface and this is the first glimpse we have of the relationship between Robbie and Cecilia which will be so important in the novel. We see this only from Cecilia's point of view here, and as she struggles to find reasons for the awkwardness between them we can't help feeling that she is avoiding confronting the obvious – that it is the attraction between them that makes them nervous in each other's presence. Her (incorrect) assumption that Robbie is unsettled by the difference in their social stations suggests her snobbishness. She is embarrassed that he has done better than her at Cambridge, and experiments with the possibility that this has made him arrogant. Her unwillingness to be drawn into a literary discussion might hint that she is aware of his superior intellect. Cecilia's fear that she has suggested a 'taste for the full-blooded and sensual' (p. 25) in her preference for Fielding over Richardson is the closest she comes to acknowledging the sexual tension between them.

A05 KEY INTERPRETATION

When Cecilia identifies her room with 'stews' on page 21, she may just mean that the room is a slovenly mess, but she would have been aware of Shakespeare's use of the word to mean a brothel. This, along with the reference to *Clarissa* (1748) by Samuel Richardson, which tells of the heroine's seduction and rape, hints at Cecilia's developing sexuality.

A04 KEY CONNECTION

The novelist and playwright Henry Fielding (1707–54) wrote boisterous and sensual novels about the (often bawdy) exploits of London characters. Some of Fielding's novels are **parodies** of Richardson's more serious works, so the fact that Cecilia claims she would rather read Fielding than Richardson may echo Cecilia's desire for fun rather than study.

PART ONE, CHAPTER THREE

Summary

- Briony struggles to get her cousins to rehearse the play.
- One of the twins, Jackson, has wet the bed and is having to wash his sheets in the laundry, which is preventing him from rehearsing. Briony, meanwhile, struggles with Pierrot's inability to intone his lines convincingly and Lola's distance. She fears that Lola thinks her childish and that she is only indulging her. She worries that 'behind her older cousin's perfect manners was a destructive intent' (p. 34).
- In a pause in rehearsals, Briony witnesses through the window the scene between Cecilia and Robbie at the fountain.
- Briony feels the urge to write an account of what she has seen, but realises she has a duty to continue rehearsals instead.
- Briony attempts to interpret the action she has seen through the window, attributing thoughts and motives to Robbie and Cecilia, but gets it horribly wrong, believing that Robbie has forced Cecilia to jump into the water. It is with some **irony** that she observes 'how easy it was to get everything wrong, completely wrong' (p. 39).

Analysis

A portrayal of adolescence

Briony's voice is used to reveal more of her character. She flits between an adolescent and a childish view and behaviour, at one moment reflecting that it is immature not to take more care of her appearance and a little later wiping her dirty hands on her white muslin dress. She is childlike as she plays with her fingers, yet more mature in her consideration of other people's minds. She recognises in herself a childish impulse to see the scene between Cecilia and Robbie as carrying some meaning for her as if it was 'a tableau mounted for her alone' (p. 39). A moment later she is quite grown-up in her acknowledgement that the scene has no meaning outside its actions, and would have taken place whether or not she were observing it. She admits to herself that 'This was not a fairy tale' (p. 40).

This retreat from seeing herself as the point or centre of the scene echoes the gradual recognition a child has that it is not, in fact, the centre of the universe for everyone else. She thinks about what it must be like to be someone else. This imaginative projection – the ability fully to imagine what it is like to be another person – is an essential skill for a writer and is a skill Briony continues to practise as a nurse in London later in the book.

KEY CONTEXT · A03

The Triton fountain in Piazza Barberini, which the Tallises' fountain is based on, was designed by Bernini in 1643. There is a dark side to its history: until the late eighteenth century, unidentified dead bodies were displayed in front of it, and the people of Rome invited to try to recognise them. The fountain in *Atonement* also has a dark role to play in Briony's story.

KEY CONTEXT · A03

Briony's consideration of other people's consciousness is a contemplation of the 'theory of mind'. This is the recognition that other people have a mind of their own, which resembles our own in many respects but is essentially distinct, and filled with their own thoughts, feelings and concerns.

Progress booster: The narrative viewpoint

Atonement's structure as a book ultimately written by Briony herself means that the narrative viewpoint is deliberately complex and troublesome. It is important that you can explore this aspect of the novel's structure with relevant quotations and examples to back up your ideas. The reader is often challenged to work out who is actually telling the story. As an adolescent, Briony already sees everything as material for her writing, and immediately ponders what use she can make of the scene she has witnessed. This is a narrative device that McEwan himself employs to add a rich complexity to the story.

Changing viewpoints

McEwan adds complexity to the structure of the novel when the narrative viewpoint draws back and we are invited to reflect on the episode from six decades in the future, with the old Briony admitting that she cannot disentangle what she thought as a child from what she has thought or written since. The **narrative** is instantly undermined, and another layer of uncertainty about what actually happened, and what it meant, is added.

As Briony stands considering that she could write a scene like the one she has just witnessed, we feel a strange lurch when we realise we are in fact reading the account she has just planned to write, and are caught up in a **reflexive**, distorted sequence. On a first reading, we are unlikely to be aware of this dislocation, but on subsequent readings it prepares the ground for a sequence of points in the novel in which the ground seems to shift under our feet. Here, the older Briony is writing about the younger Briony imagining writing the scene that the older Briony has just written.

This playing with the narratorial point of view and the **conceit** of composition engages us intellectually, disturbing the emotional engagement we are building with the voice of the young Briony. Early instances of undermining our voluntary belief in the fiction, such as this, lay the foundations for the whole-scale demolition of the literary edifice at the end of the novel. We may feel frustrated and cheated by this, as we feel we have entered into a contract with the author who is now reneging on the bargain by stepping back from a fiction that we have been led to believe in.

The poet Samuel Taylor Coleridge (1772–1834) wrote in *Biographia Literaria* (1817) of the 'willing suspension of disbelief' that allows us to believe in a fiction or poem. We know that a story is not literally 'true' but agree to believe in it to enjoy it and receive its message. McEwan arguably exploits the reader's suspension of disbelief by encouraging us to believe in the fiction and then underlining the fact that it is a fiction.

Key quotation: How a writer sees the world

Briony reflects that there is no absolute meaning in an event, but only what it means to different people. Therefore, Briony believes, as a writer, there is a need to acknowledge her characters' 'separate minds' (p. 40). This understanding of the separation between people is a key aspect of the novel. For example, Briony is forced to come to terms with the fact that her 'atonement' will never include forgiveness from Robbie Turner, because she will never be able to change his mind about her.

Revision task 1: Misinterpretations

This is the first of Briony's several misinterpretations of what she sees. What other instances of mistaken seeing are there in *Atonement*? Make brief notes on Robbie's interpretations of the other soldiers' behaviour in Dunkirk, and Emily Tallis's understanding of the Tallis household as well as any other misinterpretations you have noticed in the novel.

PART ONE, CHAPTER FOUR

Summary

- Cecilia repairs the vase and watches as Briony tears down the poster for the **melodrama**, deciding not to go ahead with the performance.
- Cecilia takes the flowers to Paul Marshall's room and through the window sees Leon Tallis and Paul Marshall arrive.
- On the way to the house Leon encounters Robbie and invites him to dinner.
- Cecilia is annoyed with Leon and wants him to rescind the invitation but Leon refuses, claiming Cecilia is being a snob; 'You think he can't hold a knife and fork' (p. 53).
- Paul tells them about his confectionery business and its success, and explains his ambitions to make money out of the widely predicted war by selling special 'Amo' bars with camouflage patterned wrappers.
- Leon and Cecilia quickly re-establish the balance of conspiracy and antagonism that marked their childhood relationship; they exchange the special 'look' that they used as a weapon as children.
- The chapter ends with the group going inside for a cocktail.

Analysis

Cecilia's thoughts

This is another chapter related from Cecilia's point of view. Again she notices and describes everything in minute detail, in the very precise, self-conscious style established in Chapter Two. The opening scene establishes the dynamic between Briony and Cecilia. Briony, tempestuous and dramatic, tears her poster but struggles not to cry, resisting the childishness of tears and cuddles. Cecilia notices with regret the indication that Briony is growing up and changing.

When Briony decides to share the reason for her temper with Cecilia, she characteristically chooses a word, 'genre' (p. 45), she has recently learnt and mispronounces it so that Cecilia does not understand her. We end up smiling at her childishness rather than recognising her maturity as she had hoped Cecilia would do. This reduction to ridicule is a technique that McEwan frequently uses to undermine Briony's self-conscious seriousness.

It is clear that, while Cecilia thinks she is disregarding Robbie, in fact he is constantly intruding into her thoughts. She has 'passed many hours deliberately not thinking about Robbie Turner' (p. 43) and even the furniture, polished by his mother, reminds her of him. Later, her anger that Leon has invited Robbie to dinner emphasises the exaggerated importance he is assuming in her thoughts.

The journey to adulthood

As Briony is embarking on adolescence, Cecilia is leaving it behind, but occasionally reverts to childish patterns of behaviour. She is too afraid of her father to confront him over the issue of smoking, and gives Leon 'the look' (p. 50). She is like a romantic teenager in the way she reflects, as she meets Paul, whether she will marry him. The reflection is not straightforward: she wonders if she will look back on this moment later, and imagines a future of happiness or disappointment stemming from it. It is one of many imagined futures in the novel.

KEY CONTEXT (A03)

'Amo' is Latin for 'I love', which is inappropriate as the name of a chocolate bar, but is probably a cynical marketing gimmick. More appositely, Paul intends to produce a version for the army, who will recognise 'amo' as an abbreviation of 'ammunition'.

Here she sees events as though fixed in the past when she contemplates the appearance of Danny Hardman, the sixteen-year-old son of Old Hardman who works on the Tallises' estate. 'All day long ... she had been ... seeing strangely, as though everything was already long in the past, made more vivid by posthumous ironies she could not quite grasp' (p. 48). McEwan uses this technique to alert us to passages and reflections that will have a bearing on later events. In this case, Cecilia's suspicion that Danny is interested in Lola is carried through to her later conviction that he was the one who attacked Lola. Again, at the end of the chapter, she feels that she is seeing everything as though it happened in the past and all outcomes are already fixed, commenting 'Whatever happened in the future, however superficially strange or shocking, would also have an unsurprising, familiar quality' (p. 53).

Paul Marshall: The 'villain' of *Atonement*?

The character of Paul Marshall is introduced and he is not **sympathetic**. He delivers a long speech about himself in which he appears to be self-important, pompous and conceited. Concentrating on his own achievements, particularly as they are in trade and commerce,

would have been considered rude at the time when the novel is set. Talking about money and commercial success was considered vulgar – a vulgarity recalled later by the appearance of the aged Paul and Lola with their expensive clothes and Lola's vivid make-up.

Paul is pompous and even ridiculous in his view of his chocolate-making as a 'purpose' and 'vision' (p. 50). The accusation of warmongering is also absurd and his repetition of it self-aggrandising. More important than these unpleasant aspects of his character, though, is the suggestion that he touches Cecilia lightly on the arm as they go into the house. She is unsure whether he has done so, and the episode is easy to overlook. But when we learn much later that it was he who assaulted Lola, the unsolicited touch looks more ominous.

A02

Progress booster: The philosophy of determinism in *Atonement*

The belief that the future is fixed, that destiny is already worked out, is called **determinism**. The philosophical debate about whether people are free to exercise their will and act as they wish, or whether all our actions are predetermined, goes back thousands of years. It is a question that Cecilia would surely have debated in her time at Cambridge. It is echoed in Cecilia's thought that 'all outcomes, on all scales – from the tiniest to the most colossal – were already in place' (p. 53). This deterministic view of events is underpinned by the poignant revelation at the end of the book that Briony is narrating the story from a future point of view in which all the events have *already* happened.

A04 KEY CONNECTION

Cecilia, Paul, Leon and Robbie are barely out of adolescence, but their choices, crimes and behaviours are to have an impact on the rest of their lives. Post-adolescent central characters featured in other texts include the character of Pinkie, seventeen-year-old ganglord in Graham Greene's *Brighton Rock* (1938), and the perpetual student and mourning son Hamlet in Shakespeare's *Hamlet* (1599).

A03 KEY CONTEXT

By 'sophisticates' (p. 46) McEwan means girls at Girton College, Cambridge, particularly those who thought themselves sophisticated. In 1935, Girton was one of only two Cambridge colleges to admit women (and not men). Women were not allowed to become full members of the University until 1948. Cecilia arguably wastes, or, at least, does not appreciate, the remarkable academic opportunity that has been given to her.

Summary

- The twins and Lola begin to get homesick and restless. The twins feel uncomfortable and shy around the other people in the house and Lola feels that this 'unstructured time oppressed them' (p. 56).

- Briony has not told Lola and the twins that she is cancelling the performance, but simply walks out without comment. They only realise that the rehearsals are ended for good when Lola wanders into Paul Marshall's (empty) room and sees Briony walking near the island.

- Jackson says 'I don't like it here' (p. 57), which seems to **foreshadow** their later attempt to run away. He says they won't ever go home because their parents are divorcing. Lola is furious with him for saying a word they had all avoided.

- Paul Marshall comes upon them at this moment of conflict. He chats to them, and produces an Amo bar from his pocket, which Lola eats.

Analysis

The development of Lola

Lola's character is developed further, reinforcing what we have seen of her already as a girl on the brink of adulthood who combines childish, adolescent and older attitudes by turns. She adopts a caring role when Jackson is unhappy, though the childish thinness of her arm undermines the gesture and makes Jackson all the sadder. She copies what we assume is her mother's behaviour in her angry response to Jackson's blunder in mentioning divorce, and in her words to Paul Marshall: 'Then I'll thank you not to talk about them in front of the children' (p. 59). The counterpoint of adult and child is most pronounced in the history of the trousers. Her story, that she bought them from Liberty's (a sophisticated adult shop) while going to London to see *Hamlet*, sounds like the actions of a grown woman. But behind the story, the reality is that she was at a matinee performance and spilt strawberry drink on her 'frock' (p. 60), so had to go to the nearest shop to buy clean clothes – a very childish scenario.

While adopting what she considers to be adult behaviour and speech, Lola is still very much a child. She flicks open a catch on Paul's suitcase, then closes it and flees. She curls her tongue around the Amo bar and gives the twins a 'serves-you-right look' as any petulant sister would. Furthermore, she panics and struggles to know what to do – has Paul heard the whole exchange about divorce? How should she respond to his comment about the papers?

Study focus: From child to adult **A05**

Notice how the mix of adult and child in Lola is apparently interesting to Paul Marshall. He has been dozing in his room, and after a dream in which his younger sisters touch his body, he wakes sexually aroused. This is a disturbing image, which does nothing to improve the poor impression we have of him. As he watches Lola curl her tongue around the Amo bar, the account is sensual and the effect on him is unnervingly sexual – 'he took a deep breath. "Bite it", he said softly. "You've got to bite it" ' (p. 62). Uncomfortably, Lola reminds him of his favourite sister (p. 61). The adult/child hybrid that excites him is clear again in the last sentence. With her mouth full of chocolate, Lola adopts the maternal tone again: 'Bath time! Run along now. Run along' (p. 62).

PART ONE, CHAPTER SIX

Summary

- The first time we meet Emily Tallis – Cecilia, Leon and Briony's mother – she is spending the afternoon in her bedroom, in the dark, fearing the onset of a migraine and 'retreating before its threat' (p. 63).
- We learn that she considers herself hampered, almost imprisoned, by the 'knifing pains' (p. 63) of migraine.
- She spends some considerable time planning what she will do when she is out of the room, and then delays her emergence further by deciding to search for dark glasses and flat shoes so that she can go outside to look for Briony.

Analysis

Emily Tallis: A weak mother

Through Emily's own voice, we learn a great deal about her character in this chapter. It is significant that she has not featured in the book so far – her retreat from the family and the house outside her room is mirrored in her late arrival in the plot. She likes to feel that she is a central, coordinating force, but in fact she appears to be redundant in a household that runs itself without her. Her one clear act so far has been to order a roast dinner, a meal which is highly inappropriate on such a hot day and which is causing strife in the kitchen. The room is almost an extension of herself as she notices the creaks and strains of the building, 'the rafters and posts drying out' (p. 64), with the same attentiveness she devotes to monitoring the state of her own body, teetering on the brink of a migraine.

She has an indulgent, romantic view of Briony, whom she describes as 'the softest little thing' (p. 65), and a sentimental view of herself as a mother who is plagued by her 'habitual fretting' (p. 66). She is already nostalgic for the time when Briony was smaller and considers herself to have been at her best and most sparkling when with her. Despite what she says, the history she describes reveals that she has been at best ineffectual, and at worst neglectful, as a mother. She says that she has 'longed to rise up and intervene, especially if she thought Briony was in need of her' (pp. 66–7), but the fear of pain has stood in her way. She lists a string of domestic chores she will carry out ahead of finding and comforting Briony.

Key quotation: Emily's misguided view of Paul   **A01**

Hearing a 'little squeal of laughter abruptly smothered' (p. 69) Emily assumes this is innocent activity between Paul and Lola and an indication that he 'might not be such a bad sort' (p. 69) if he is prepared to amuse children. The action between Paul and Lola is taking place after the twins have gone to their bath, and results in Lola's injuries. This reminds the reader of Emily's lack of real knowledge of what is happening in the house around her, as well as providing another example of a disastrous misunderstanding.

Revision task 2: Depictions of pain   **A02**

Atonement has many descriptions of illness and injury. Find some examples of McEwan describing characters in pain and make notes on the kind of imagery and language McEwan uses to convey their experiences.

PART ONE, CHAPTER SEVEN

Summary

- The action of the novel has now reverted to the moments before the arrival of Leon and Paul Marshall.
- Briony has gone to the ruined temple on the island and is venting her frustration by attacking stinging nettles with a peeled hazel switch. She imagines that they represent her cousins and punishes them for spoiling her play.
- She then turns on playwriting as her victim, and finally the earlier stages of her childhood, in an act of 'self-purification' (p. 74) to make way for her new, older self. Leon approaches in the trap, but she refuses to acknowledge him. Briony instead waits on the bridge for something to happen.

Analysis

Briony's reverie

McEwan returns to Briony's point of view in this chapter and we see what she has been doing while the twins and Lola were talking to Paul Marshall. Briony's anger has given way to indulgent and enjoyable destruction. She has taken the time to peel a stick before launching an assault on the nettles and finds the activity satisfying. Typically, her imagination takes over and she makes a **narrative** of what she is doing. The depiction of the scene is benign, and the venom with which she assaults nettles representing Lola is arguably disarmed by the childish context, even though the language is violent: 'the singing arc of a three-foot switch cut her down at the knees' (p. 74). Briony, as a child herself, has no real violent intent towards Lola and, in fact, Lola appears to get her own back when the nettles 'sting her toes' (p. 74).

This activity leads Briony into an even more childish reverie, or dream, as she imagines herself lauded as a world champion nettle-slasher at the Olympic Games. In conjuring up this picture she adopts the terms of a sports commentator, analysing her movements and technique.

We have the sense of her being watched, or watching herself, and imagining the impact on others or how she would be described. She is disappointed that Leon does not stop the trap and speak to her. Even though she had anticipated having to 'suffer the interruption with good grace' (p. 75), she was secretly hoping he would stop, as this would demonstrate interest in her. Her happy picture of her activity deflates and she becomes 'a solitary girl swiping nettles with a stick' (p. 76), robbed of any significance. She is struck by the futility of her activity but also of all she can do; her circumstances are frustratingly limited.

Study focus: An ominous ending

A05

By the end of the chapter, Briony has lapsed into petulance. She is once again the child demanding to be noticed, hoping to be the centre of someone's universe, but with the growing and annoying recognition that she is not: 'She would simply wait on the bridge, calm and obstinate, until events, real events, not her own fantasies, rose to her challenge, and dispelled her insignificance' (p. 77). Her challenge will be met the same evening by the events that unfold, and Briony's desire to be important will be the catalyst for disaster.

KEY CONTEXT   A03

The temple is the ruin of a neoclassical folly – a building intended largely to decorate the landscape, built in the style of classical Greek or Roman architecture and popular on country estates in the mid and late eighteenth century. It is **symbolic** in *Atonement* of the declining upper-middle-class lifestyle that the Tallises still uphold. Significantly, it is replaced by a functional 'wooden bench, and a litter basket' (p. 363) at the end of the novel.

KEY INTERPRETATION   A05

Writing about the impact of quantum physics on the intellectual landscape of the twentieth century, McEwan has said: 'The observer is a part of what he observes. Reality is changed by the presence of the observer – he can no longer pretend to be invisible' (introduction to *Or Shall We Die?* (Jonathan Cape, 1983), p. 17).

PART ONE, CHAPTER EIGHT

Summary

- Robbie has returned home and bathed, and the chapter opens with him looking at the landscape in the fading evening light. The house is small and cramped, and we feel aware of his bulk crammed into the tiny room in contrast to the open spaces of the garden and the Tallises' house.
- He runs over in his mind Cecilia's undressing and plunge into the pool, realising that, although he has never thought about her as anything other than a childhood companion, he is now drawn to her sexually, and visualises her in detail, 'a drop of water on her upper arm' (p. 79). Deducing that Cecilia will be unhappy that he is coming to dinner, he drafts a letter to her.
- He makes several attempts before successfully typing a letter that he feels has the right balance of seriousness and levity, admitting he feels 'light-headed' (p. 85) around Cecilia. Then he spontaneously types an obscene ending to his letter and rips it from the typewriter.
- Robbie rewrites the letter, without the obscenities, and then gets dressed for dinner.
- Robbie walks slowly to the Tallis house, contemplating the happy future he envisages as a successful and cultured doctor. It is a sad **irony** that he is so certain of this ideal future but, as we later discover, will not live to enjoy it. On the way to the hall, he finds Briony waiting on the bridge and gives her the letter to take ahead to Cecilia.
- Too late, Robbie realises he has left the good copy of the letter at home and has put the obscene copy in the envelope that Briony has taken.

Analysis

Robbie's point of view

The chapter opens with a new voice, but it is not until the second paragraph that we discover it belongs to Robbie. It is clearly an educated and cultured voice, mentioning poets such as W. H. Auden, Keats, Petrarch and A. E. Housman, Shakespeare's *Twelfth Night* (in which Robbie took the part of Malvolio – significantly, a character who is doomed to humiliation following a misunderstanding in love). This chapter is important in revealing Robbie's character and fills in his background to give a fuller view of his personality and how it has developed.

Robbie is learning medical terminology – 'capitate, hamate, triquetral' (p. 82) – and his desire to learn and develop himself is clearly very strong. This could be evidence of his greater accomplishment, which gave him a first-class degree and Cecilia only a third. His voice and character are important, as he will relate the second part of the book.

Robbie's feelings about Cecilia

Robbie's reflections on the incident with Cecilia reveal not only to us but also to himself how his feelings about her have changed. He contemplates the irony that he has spent three years studying classical love poetry at university as if feelings of love were just 'symptoms' and writing about love contained not much more than 'literary conventions' (p. 84). He now pictures himself as one of these **Romantic poets**, or 'some ruffed and plumed courtier' (p. 84), who worship their loved one. There is a sense that Robbie is wryly criticising himself.

A03 KEY CONTEXT

Fauvism (p. 78) was an artistic movement, led by Henri Matisse (1869–1954), which flourished at the turn of the twentieth century. Fauvists used brilliantly coloured paints applied directly from the tube to achieve astonishing boldness and vibrancy. The 'wildness' in their art may reflect the heightened emotions felt by Robbie at this time.

A03 KEY CONTEXT

Gray's Anatomy is a definitive text on anatomy by Henry Gray (1825–61), first published in 1858. It has been through many editions since. The illustration referred to as number 1236 was in fact not labelled as such until the 1962 edition. This would have been easy for McEwan to check, so is perhaps one of Briony's errors and evidence of a reworking of the novel in the 1960s.

KEY CONTEXT   **A03**

The influential literary critic F. R. Leavis (1895–1978) (p. 91) taught English at Cambridge from 1925 to 1962. He introduced a new, serious style of literary criticism that required critics to look at the life and moral opinions of the writer. He was a demanding and severe teacher. This reflects the high quality of Robbie's literary education, which he is considering rejecting for a career in medicine.

Unlike Briony, who waits for something to happen, Robbie takes decisive action in writing to Cecilia. This decisiveness will stand him in good stead during the coming war. After the careful control when phrasing his letter, he lets his real feelings come out in the obscene ending he adds to the typed version. Although Robbie refers to Sigmund Freud a few times in interpreting his own actions, he states that putting the wrong letter into the envelope doesn't need to be analysed in this way. His denial immediately suggests the opposite to us – that this was subconsciously deliberate, to precipitate a crisis with Cecilia which gives him the chance to act and know her feelings.

Progress booster: Social class in *Atonement*   **A02**

It is important to think about the way McEwan presents the English class system in *Atonement*, and the effects of the Second World War on the social-class structure. In a novel in which the links between events over time are such an important theme, it is not surprising that we see how Robbie's character has been forged from events in his earlier life and the resulting way in which he has travelled between different social classes, literally 'moving freely between the bungalow and the main house' (p. 86). His mother is the Tallises' cleaning lady, which makes him lower working class, and his father abandoned the family when he was young. The Tallises have paid for Robbie to go to university and treat him as the son of their upper-class family, saving his mother from what she sees as a 'pinched life' (p. 88) as a penniless single mother. Cecilia is sometimes snobbish towards him and avoids him when they are both at university, but their love ultimately transcends social class. Briony's account of Cecilia and Robbie's down-at-heel flat in London (even if this is not where they ultimately ended up) conveys a sense that being of either upper or lower social class is now unimportant to them – they are now plainly living as a soldier and a nurse.

We are told that Robbie is 'without social unease' (p. 86) and McEwan gives us examples of how he has confounded people's expectations of his class. Though Cecilia thought he removed his shoes to make a point about social status, he says he did it to avoid treading on the floor Polly had just cleaned, and then removed his socks in case they were smelly. The implication is that Cecilia is more aware of the class difference, and Robbie doesn't care about it. Robbie is respected as if he is an officer by his fellow soldiers in France, and it is suggested that his class is defined more by his intelligence and leadership than by family background.

As a counterpoint to Robbie, McEwan uses Paul Marshall as an example of how having social advantages and immense wealth can bring a person power and prestige despite being a rapist. Marshall thrives throughout the war and beyond, continuing to actually climb the social-class ladder and becoming Lord Marshall by the end of the novel. In contrast, the Tallis family decline and the family home becomes a hotel.

Key quotation: A woman's role?   **A01**

Emily Tallis, as an upper-class woman of the early twentieth century, does not believe that women should work at all; in her mind Cecilia's main goals in life should be 'a husband to find and motherhood to confront' (p. 65). However, Briony and Cecilia have a very different view of their future lives – no longer content with the privileged and indolent life of the upper-class wife, they map out their futures as university graduates, both training to be nurses, and Briony a life as a writer.

PART ONE, CHAPTER NINE

Summary

- The **narrative** switches back to Cecilia who is unsettled, changing her dress twice before she is satisfied with her appearance, which she sees distorted and 'Picasso-like' (p. 99) in her mirror.

- On the way out of her room for the last time, she is surprised by Jackson and is side-tracked into sorting out the twins' problem of having only one pair of socks between them, although she is 'gratified' (p. 99) by their need for her help.

- In the kitchen, she mediates between her mother and the cook, arguing over Emily's desire to cancel the roast dinner and make salad. Emily Tallis's interference has reduced Betty the cook to 'fury' (p. 104) and conveys her ineptitude as matriarch of the house. Free at last to drink gin and tonic with her brother Leon on the terrace, Cecilia talks nervously with him, finding it difficult to move beyond their childhood relationship. Briony avoids her mother's attempt to send her away to clean up and passes Robbie's note to Cecilia.

- Cecilia takes in the message, including the obscene postscript, without betraying any surprise or shock. But she quickly realises that Robbie would not have sent it as a folded note and that Briony has read it.

Analysis

Another glimpse of Cecilia

This chapter reveals more of Cecilia's character. She sees herself as essential to managing and soothing the household. She feels obliged to help the twins, she negotiates for the cook, finding a solution that does not undermine or embarrass her mother, and intends also to look for Briony – 'Someone else to worry about' (p. 101). Cecilia detects no **irony** in Leon's comment on her adopting the role of mother as it matches her own view of herself.

Cecilia slips back into her habitual way of relating to Leon and there is little evidence of the sophistication she claims to have developed at Cambridge. She adores him, and sees him as suave, relaxed, carefree – though to us he appears shallow with only superficial interests and a dull life as a banker. She is anxious and unsure, overcompensating by trying to be witty, but is aware that she is not coming across well, and is self-conscious. She admits that she is 'influenced by Leon's tone' (p. 109) but her self-mockery is painful and lacks conviction.

Key quotation: Cecilia understands her feelings **(A01)**

After reading Robbie's note, Cecilia quickly recognises her own feelings for Robbie. The words 'Of course, of course' (p. 111) repeat themselves in her mind. She deduces that an unacknowledged interest in him has worked subconsciously to keep her near him but made her encounters with him awkward.

Revision task 3: Keeping up appearances **(A02)**

Despite the strong language of the note, Cecilia is able to maintain an 'expression of amused curiosity' (p. 111). Make notes on other instances in the book when characters such as Robbie and Lola do not reveal their true feelings.

(A04) KEY CONNECTION

The twins Pierrot and Jackson, and their sister Lola, are rather lonely and ignored children, with disastrous consequences. McEwan's portrayal of childhood and his consideration of what children need from the adults around them also echo the lonely and abused Louise Gradgrind in *Hard Times* (1854) by Charles Dickens.

(A03) KEY CONTEXT

One of the most complete examples of neo-Gothic architecture is Strawberry Hill, the house of eccentric parliamentarian Horace Walpole who wrote one of the first Gothic novels in the English language, *The Castle of Otranto* (1764). Cecilia regards the 'neo-Gothic' of the Tallis house as a 'sham' (p. 102), the setting underlining the theme of artifice in the novel.

Summary

- Briony mulls over the obscene word in the letter, relishing her feeling of disgust. She wonders how to write about what has happened and the new, adult insight into life it has given her.
- She drifts into a meditation on writing and what it requires, reflecting that she can describe things well but needs to learn how to capture and show emotions.
- Lola comes in and shows Briony the scratches and scrapes that she says the twins have inflicted on her. Briony feels the grown-up responsibility to console her. In an attempt to look mature herself Briony tells Lola about the letter, pleased with the shocked reaction it elicits. The two encourage each other in working up Robbie as a threat and a 'maniac' (p. 119), a word that Briony finds very appealing.
- On the way down to dinner, Briony goes to the library where she makes out two figures in the dark. At first she wonders if she imagines them, but then recognises Cecilia and Robbie. She misinterprets their stance and thinks Robbie is attacking Cecilia. She stares in shock, not knowing what to do, until Cecilia eventually straightens her clothes and walks past Briony, out of the room.
- Briony follows her sister, certain that she has rescued her from a dangerous assault.

Analysis

Lies, pretence and misinterpretation

By the end of this chapter, the misconceptions that will spiral irrevocably to the crisis of the novel are in place and the action takes on a fatal inevitability from this point.

Briony shows awareness of the way in which reading the note and being an observer of Robbie and Cecilia's relationship are taking her to areas of thought she had never considered before – as she says 'an arena of adult emotion and dissembling' (p. 113). The notion of 'dissembling' is complex – it can be defined as 'lying' but can also be more subtle: deception, bluffing, saving face and pretending can all be called dissembling, and Briony has witnessed Cecilia and Robbie clearly pretending outwardly that there is nothing unusual between them.

KEY INTERPRETATION A05

A good introduction to McEwan's writing is Sebastian Groes's *Ian McEwan: Contemporary Critical Perspectives*, second edition (Bloomsbury Academic, 2013).

KEY CONNECTION A04

Misdelivered, rewritten letters and other types of communication are a common literary device, and can be found in Shakespeare's *Hamlet* (1599) and, in the form of a privately recorded vinyl single, in Graham Greene's *Brighton Rock* (1938). Letters and pens are also significant in the plot of Agatha Christie's *The Murder of Roger Ackroyd* (1926).

Study focus: The nature of authorship

A05

This chapter is important in developing Briony's character as well as the action. Her image of herself as a writer is very much in the foreground, and the theme of writing is explored further through this. The young Briony makes the link between 'dissembling' and the fictional world of writing, and so she takes inspiration from what is happening around her. Futhermore, as Briony mulls over the obscene word Robbie has used, not everything passing through her mind is convincing for a child of thirteen. She deduces the meaning of the word from a context that is distinctly adult, and demonstrates anatomical knowledge that is not consistent with her claim that not even her mother had ever mentioned that part of the body. We might feel that the voice of the older Briony breaks through the **narrative** here. When reading *Atonement*, be aware that McEwan presents characters lying and playing roles throughout the novel and that Briony's retrospective authorship of the text is also part of the misinterpretation of events.

What is reality?

Briony comments that she is quite able to capture the reality of things in description, but struggles to convey emotion rather than state it: 'how was [sadness itself] put across so it could be felt in all its lowering immediacy?' (p. 116). This is a common theme of creative-writing courses and seems to belong more to the later writer than to the thirteen-year-old Briony.

Again, Briony feels that she is leaving childhood behind and is being initiated into an adult world of mysteries that she can't quite grasp but must come to terms with if she is to write successfully. She decides she must reject the simple, clear morality familiar to her from children's books. However, this is precisely what she returns to in damning Robbie and reconsidering her previous encounters with him in the light of what she thinks she has discovered. She and Lola indulge in a childish frenzy of overdramatising events and working Robbie up as a terrible and dangerous villain. It is in this overwrought state, with her imagination running away with her, that she comes across the lovers in the library and sees what she expects to see – an unwelcome assault rather than a shared moment of passion.

Briony's desire for drama in her life, which has been clear from the start of the book, makes her fix eagerly on the supposed threat of Robbie. What could have been comical as a juvenile misunderstanding of adult passion is dangerously distorted by her desire for drama, sensation and attention. By chance, it becomes the catalyst for disaster.

A03 KEY CONTEXT

'There was an old lady who swallowed a fly' (p. 115) is a line from a comic song. An old lady swallows a fly, then a spider to eat it, then a bird to eat the spider, and so on until she dies after eating a horse. The parallel is clear – a simple, harmless occurrence sets in motion a train of events that snowballs, ending in catastrophe because of an inappropriate reaction.

PART ONE, CHAPTER ELEVEN

Summary

- The guests are stifled by the heat. Dinner is awkward, marred by aggressive remarks and suppressed feelings.
- Robbie recalls events since his arrival at the house: explaining his mistake to Cecilia, making love in the library and being interrupted by Briony. Cecilia is also preoccupied by her thoughts.
- The twins leave the table and Briony reveals the scratches and bruises they have supposedly inflicted on Lola.
- Emily's inability to make the social situation run smoothly means that it gets off to a slow start.
- Briony discovers a note the twins have left, saying they are running away. The party breaks up as all, except Emily, set out to search for the boys. Robbie searches alone.

Analysis

An uncomfortable atmosphere

The atmosphere in the dining room is stifling – both from the physical heat and from the emotions held in check. Paul's sickly cocktail, the inappropriate warm dessert and the obligation to eat too much contribute to the suffocating fullness of the scene. In the room, as with the food and drinks, excess and extravagance are cloying and irritating. This mirrors the way the novel is building up. There has been a run of small incidents, blown out of proportion by the characters but with an impact that has been contained, giving a sense of building pressure. Robbie describes the conversation as full of 'harmless inanities' (p. 130). Some cool, fresh relief is needed to counteract the heat of the evening. McEwan builds the pressure through the details of the over-rich food, the suppressed love-making in the library and the squabbling during the evening meal.

An intimate memory

While the diners eat, Robbie recollects the interval in the library with Cecilia. He recalls very precisely, with evocative description, exactly how he felt, what her body was like and what they did, 'her arms were looped around his head' (p. 135). The level of detail is surprising, even shocking, in its intimacy. The episode of passion is given extended treatment as it is to be the only one they can enjoy, and memories of it must sustain both the lovers through Robbie's imprisonment and the war. We need this level of detail in order to understand what it is that Robbie recreates in Part Two of the novel.

The first attack on Lola

Lola's injuries, revealed to the table by Briony, are still presented as though inflicted by the twins, and Emily comments in shock 'you're bruised up to your elbows' (p. 141). There are clues for us that the twins did not cause the bruising. At the time when Lola claimed the twins attacked her, we saw her letting them into the room and talking to them. They told Cecilia they were afraid to ask Lola to help them find socks, and it seemed 'wondrous' (p. 118) to Briony that the twins could have upset Lola so much. Paul, who is also scratched, says that he had to pull the twins off Lola – yet we saw the whole of his encounter with Lola and the twins and this did not happen.

KEY CONNECTION — A04

The line 'nothing that can be can come between me and the full prospect of my hopes' (p. 131) is a quotation from Shakespeare's *Twelfth Night* (III.4.81–2). Malvolio says this when anticipating consummation of his desire for Olivia, but he is thwarted. The use of this quotation in Robbie's thoughts here tells us that, although the consummation of their desire looks inevitable, things can (and will) still go wrong. There are several references and **allusions** to *Twelfth Night* in *Atonement*.

PROGRESS BOOSTER — A02

Look at the language McEwan uses on page 125 to build up the atmosphere of stifled tension. Think about:

- The effect of verbs such as 'nauseated' and 'warped'
- The uncomfortable aspects of the social rules and expectations, such as the choice of drinks and food items

Summary

- Emily Tallis has remained in the house, certain the twins will return on their own.

- She is resentful that Lola appears to want to be the centre of attention, in the same way that Lola's mother always wanted attention – this brings up an 'old antagonism' (p. 146) in Emily. She mourns the imminent end of Briony's childhood.

- Emily's thoughts turn to her husband. He is clearly having an affair, but she does not want to confront him. She is content to wait until, in old age, he returns to her. Her misunderstanding of his life is shown by the way she considers the war preparation work he is doing at the ministry to be 'silly' (p. 150).

- When Jack Tallis telephones, he is displeased that she has not called the police; he does so himself.

- The conversation between Emily and her husband is interrupted by the arrival of Cecilia, Leon, Briony and Lola, in distress. Leon speaks to his father but will not immediately tell Emily what has happened.

Study focus: The inability to act **AO2**

Emily Tallis is almost incapable of action of any kind. By her own confession, her life has turned out to be 'massive and empty' (p. 151) as she has wasted it on superficialities. As her musings wander between topics, she reveals that she will not confront her husband about the affair she knows he is having, and we have already seen her fail to have any effect on the household. Her inertia extends to what she expects of others and how she views their behaviour. She believes preparations for a possible war are overdramatising the risk, that Jack should not interfere in Robbie's life by paying for his education, and even that Robbie's plans for the garden are pointless as she will be dead before the plants have grown to an appreciable size. Think about the way in which inaction has an effect on characters – such as Briony's inaction in the face of her lies, and Cecilia's inaction at Briony's confession in the third part of the novel.

Key quotation: Mr and Mrs Tallis **AO1**

McEwan describes Jack Tallis as 'the senior Civil Servant' (p. 154), conveying his considerable instrumental power even at a distance. In contrast, Emily senses Leon's news could 'have her collapsing on the tiles and cracking her head' (p. 155), with her feelings characteristically focused on herself rather than the other characters.

AO3 KEY CONTEXT

By 1935, most people thought that war in Europe was inevitable. Emily's refusal to think about the threat or take seriously the projections of casualties is characteristic of her.

AO3 KEY CONTEXT

The phrase 'Ploughshares into tinfoil' (p. 153) comes from a verse in the Bible: 'Beat your plowshares into swords, and your pruning hooks into spears' (Joel 3:10). Jack Tallis is being dismissive of Paul Marshall's ambition here, suggesting he is using valuable resources to make something useless. A ploughshare is the blade of a plough that cuts through the earth.

PART ONE, CHAPTER THIRTEEN

Summary

- Briony sees her mother lying on the couch inside and spies on her briefly. Emily looks old and tired, leading Briony to imagine her funeral. She considers going in, but decides instead to head off to the island.

- A few times on the way she almost turns back, as it is so dark, but in the end she presses ahead. She hears a cry from the bridge, which at first she imagines is a startled duck, and only later realises was human.

- She is strangely unperturbed by the apparent movement of the bush, which draws her attention to Lola and another figure. When she disturbs them, Lola speaks and the unidentified person walks away.

- Much is made of how little Briony can make out in the darkness, even though she claims 'She had no doubt' (p. 165). All this is set to undermine Briony's later certainty.

- As Briony soothes Lola, she suggests explanations to her – Lola says very little herself. Briony convinces herself that Lola has been attacked by Robbie and persuades Lola that she saw him.

- Pleased to adopt the role of mature helper, Briony launches enthusiastically into the task of comforting Lola and helping her to the house, until Leon and Cecilia meet them and Leon carries Lola back.

- The **narrator** reflects on the way these catastrophic, life-changing events would be 'pursued as demons in private for many years afterwards' (p. 167).

Analysis

A search in the dark

Here the **narrative** moves back in time again to Briony's search for the twins. She goes through the motions of looking for the twins but is confident they will be safe. She enjoys the chance to practise describing the episode in her writing, imagining the twins floating face down in the pool, and reflects again on how she is crossing the border into adulthood, commenting, 'Wasn't writing a kind of soaring, an achievable form of flight, of fancy, of the imagination?' (p. 157). She revels in Robbie's hatred and imagines what else might be happening in the darkness and how her own future might unfold. At one point she hears a shout in the distance and sees a torch flash on and off – later we might wonder if this was perhaps part of the incident between Paul and Lola, or just an innocent part of the search, and this contributes to a sense of both wilful and accidental misinterpretations of events.

Study focus: The ebb and flow of time

A02

Note how the **chronological account** is interfered with by this chapter, which is itself set earlier than the end of the previous chapter. It opens with a leap into the future, referring to Briony's crime yet to be committed. This piques our interest – we have now heard so much about an ensuing disaster that we are keen to find out what it is and welcome this reassurance that it will be revealed soon. This continues a pattern already established in the narrative of moving backwards and forwards through time to manipulate our expectations and responses. This is also a typical structural feature of modernist novels of the type that Briony so admires.

KEY CONTEXT   **A03**

The **modernist** writing of the early decades of the twentieth century has impressed Briony. However, we might suspect McEwan of suggesting that Briony is being naive when, for example, she firmly embraces the modernist idea that characters and plots 'were quaint devices that belonged to the nineteenth century' (p. 281). There is evidence that McEwan believes plots are important in novels when we remember that McEwan calls *Atonement* his 'Northanger Abbey' – a novel that presents a highly plotted structure with a series of misunderstandings, just like *Atonement*.

A world of the imagination

Briony is preoccupied with her own concerns – with how she feels she is growing up, and how she can turn experiences into literature. Her fertile imagination builds potential narratives and possible futures from any scrap of event or fleeting thought. These fantasies combine her desire for excitement, her literary ambitions (she ponders how she will write about them) and her need for attention. In considering her mother's funeral she stresses that 'It had to be witnessed' (p. 162). This is the same desire to see others seeing her that Cecilia has exhibited earlier.

As Briony draws towards the island and her discovery of Lola, there are many overt reminders that events could have gone differently – that she might have turned back, that she could have stayed in the room with her mother – and then the crisis would have been averted. The slightest reasons impel events in the particular direction they finally take – Robbie's decision to search alone, Briony's reluctance to explain why she was looking through the window, her unwillingness to give in to fear and her desire to appear grown-up.

Children and adults

On pages 167–71, in the space between the repetition of the words 'I can. And I will', the inevitability of all that follows is spelt out. The certainty in those words, though ill-founded, seals the fate of all the characters involved. We see forward to the future weeks during which Briony sticks to her story and Lola remains silent. The blameworthiness of Briony in particular, but also of Lola, is held up to scrutiny – Briony was only a child, she was not helped to re-examine her story, but felt only encouragement to stick with it. She would feel the disapproval of adults if she faltered in her certainty and, for a child like Briony, desperate for adult attention and to feel important, this was certain to make her ignore any doubts and follow the path mapped out for her.

How clearly can we see?

This chapter is remarkable for the great emphasis it places on description and the visual, especially as it takes place in the dark. We end the chapter with a clear sense that we have seen exactly what has been going on – recreating in us the same error that Briony commits of trusting what we have imagined as a representation of the truth. Even elements of the description which stress how little is visible have their own visual precision: 'the dark disc of Lola's face showed nothing at all' (p. 167).

A04 KEY CONNECTION

McEwan shows a catastrophe precipitated by a seemingly insignificant act or decision in many of his works. For example, in *The Child in Time* (1987), a father's moment of inattention leads to his daughter's permanent disappearance. In S. T. Coleridge's *The Rime of the Ancient Mariner* (1789), the shooting of the albatross precedes a devastating sequence of disasters.

Revision task 4: Considering Lola **A05**

Make notes on the way McEwan presents Lola throughout the novel. Think about the following questions:

● How culpable is Lola in the tragic events that take place in the novel?

● How might it be possible to have different responses to Lola?

EXTRACT ANALYSIS: CHAPTER THIRTEEN (PP. 168–9)

Here we are presented with a description of the investigation into the rape of Lola. It is compressed into a short, vital passage of reflection. Briony's doubts about what she saw are acknowledged, and we see the process by which these doubts were quashed or ignored at the time.

The image of the 'glazed surface' of Briony's conviction with 'hairline cracks' (p. 168) recalls the Meissen vase, mended so that the cracks are barely visible. Both the vase and Briony's story will come apart again later. It recalls, too, the flaw in the bowl in Henry James's novel *The Golden Bowl* (1904).

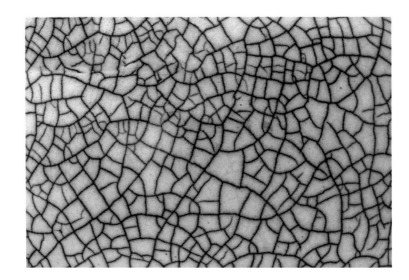

In acknowledging that she did not really see Robbie, but 'knew' (p. 169) it was him, Briony falls short of admitting that she lied. As a child, she believed in her strange means of perception. Indeed, her mother has been shown to have a similar faith in intuitive knowledge. Sitting silently in the house, Emily feels and senses what is going on around her, and 'what she knew, she knew' (p. 66). Briony sees what she expects to see: 'The truth instructed her eyes' (p. 169). This is a **motif** repeated throughout the novel, but it never has such dire consequences as here.

Briony interprets events so that they fulfil a pattern she has seen and wants to complete. She believes that symmetry and common sense confirm what she knows and that this in itself is evidence. We have already seen that she hates disorder. She will not write about divorce

because it is messy. She will not violate symmetry in her own stories, and does not like to think it can be violated in real life. She has already wondered how to use the scene at the fountain in her writing. Now she is going beyond using experience to form stories, and is using story to recast experience.

The passage is presented as though it is a mirror on Briony's reflections at the time, though clearly it has been refracted through years of guilt and analysis of what she did. The writing makes excuses for her as she might have done herself: 'What she meant was rather more complex'; 'There were no opportunities, no time' (p. 169). There is a childish image of scary things emerging from the quiet village, something frightening and powerful that had been waiting for this catastrophe. She is overly defensive, voicing a childish desire to avoid blame, but there is also a more adult point to this, examining psychological motives. Briony as a child was eager to please, afraid of upsetting people, scared to change her version of events because she was nervous of disapproval or getting into trouble. This is convincing, and prepares the way for the courage she shows later in deciding to retract her statement. The recriminations will be far greater if she changes it in the future. She feels foolish if she deviates from her story as older, more experienced people show displeasure; it is 'wise' (p. 169) brows that frown. This extended explanation generates some sympathy for Briony. It is easy to understand a person, especially a child, being afraid to disappoint people and to get herself into trouble.

The final image, of the 'bride-to-be' (p. 169) who has doubts before a wedding, prefigures Lola's wedding to Paul in Part Three. Did Lola have doubts? At the same time, it recalls the marriage-centred plot of *The Trials of Arabella* and the unsatisfactory marriages of the novel so far. Instead of the appealing, foolish nervousness the comparison might be expected to conjure up, any reflection on marriage as it is presented in *Atonement* would suggest that doubts are highly appropriate.

The passage concentrates solely on Briony's actions and reactions. Her excitement, her desire to find or impose a satisfying pattern on events, and her fear of alienating people by expressing her doubts are all given as reasons for her to remain loyal to her story. The great absence in all of this is Lola. Everything put in motion by Briony could have been stopped by Lola, and why it is not remains a mystery. It could be argued that Lola's silence is by far the worse crime. The fact that Lola's motivations are not discussed comes down to a question of ownership: 'It was [Briony's] story, the one that was writing itself around her' (p. 166).

A03 KEY CONTEXT

Briony writes *The Trials of Arabella* very much with Leon in mind, as a lesson in how to choose his bride, but ends up writing her novel as an act of atonement. Robbie, Cecilia and Briony frequently refer to literature they have read to make sense of their lives. Make notes on the role of literature in *Atonement*.

A04 KEY CONNECTION

On page 204, Robbie gives a list of figures from literature to which he compares himself and Cecilia. All are couples for whom love does not go smoothly. Only Emma and George Knightley, from Jane Austen's *Emma* (1816), are happily united at the end of their story. This is another example of love across the ages being a significant theme in *Atonement*.

PART ONE, CHAPTER FOURTEEN

Summary

- Lola is led upstairs sobbing. The police arrive. Briony relates her version of events, saying that she saw Robbie. The family doctor arrives to examine Lola.
- Downstairs, everyone but Cecilia talks in small groups; Cecilia is angry and upset, and stands apart smoking.
- Remembering Robbie's note, Briony rushes to find it, then gives it to the policeman. Cecilia is furious when she discovers that everyone has read it and storms off to her room.
- Briony gives her first official statement. She shows the positions in which she saw Robbie and Cecilia in the library, and insists again that she definitely saw Robbie on the island.
- However, very late into the night, Robbie appears through the morning mist carrying one of the twins on his shoulders and accompanied by the other. Briony is sent indoors before he arrives at the house. She is incensed that he may be hailed as a hero and her own actions forgotten.
- From her room, Briony sees Robbie taken away, handcuffed, in the police car. Still firm in her belief that she understands all she sees, Briony interprets Cecilia's last exchange with Robbie as generous forgiveness, whereas we later learn it is a declaration of loyalty and love.
- As the car leaves, Robbie's mother, Grace, appears on the drive to stand in front of it. She launches an assault, screaming that they are all liars, and hitting the car with an umbrella. Robbie is driven away.

Analysis

The aftermath of the attack

The chapter opens with a glimpse of the future, showing how Briony will later be tortured by remorse as a result of what happened in the immediate aftermath of the attack. It is the night of the attack and the early morning that followed that will trouble her more than the legal processes that will unfold in the subsequent weeks. The rest of the chapter sets out how this future situation will come about.

For the first time in the novel, a great deal of action takes place – Briony's desire for excitement has been fulfilled. She revels in being centre stage, with a feeling akin to the 'Christmas morning sensation' (p. 177).

The chapter is sprinkled with doubt about the older Briony's memories of events. She questions how she can remember seeing the doctor arrive when she knows that she must have been in another room with her mother, for instance. The doubt of the older Briony casts the certainty of her former self into relief.

Briony justifies her actions

Briony tries hard to convince herself, as well as the police and her family, of what she saw. Her motive for doing this is not malice against Robbie, but a desire for a neat story, to see things work out as she feels they should to create a **narrative** with integrity. She does not pause, at

---

KEY CONTEXT (A03)

Psychological studies have shown that people may often build false memories. The psychologist Jean Piaget (1896–1980) described an example of this, explaining how our minds may store accounts we hear of events but later recall them as though they were real memories. Briony has previously said (p. 41) that she thinks she recalls her own retelling of events rather than original experience.

this age, to reflect that life is not a balanced narrative, and in trying to impose one she wrecks the lives of the people she uses as characters.

It is partly to bolster her own certainty that Briony rushes to find Robbie's letter. **Ironically**, handing over the letter gives her a feeling of doing good, yet a motivating factor is 'that [it] could only earn her praise' (p. 177). Her desire to remain the star of the scene is strongly underlined by her private fury that Robbie should turn up with the twins. She fears that he will be lauded as a hero and that she will be overshadowed.

Grace Turner's outburst, 'Liars! Liars!' (p. 187), as the police take Robbie away, is heart-wrenching to read. We know she is right and Robbie is innocent, but this scene is related dispassionately by Briony. She does not allow herself to consider Grace's agony – she so far has no capacity to fully imagine herself in someone else's position. Our own response, though, is of immense sympathy for Grace and a sudden, devastating recognition of the distance between the drama as Briony is seeing it and the terrible reality for Robbie and Grace. The result is a more poignant rendering of the moment than would have been achieved by any expression of sympathy from Briony, the **narrator**.

Progress booster: Writing about minor characters

(A02)

Atonement has a small cast of 'main characters' (the Tallis family, Robbie Turner and the Marshalls) but a more detailed knowledge of the novel should include being able to understand and evaluate the role of the minor characters. In this section of the book Grace Turner, Robbie's mother, has an interesting role in relation to the Tallis family. 'Charlady', 'occasional clairvoyant' (p. 86) and wife to the Tallises' former gardener, the mysterious Ernest Turner, Grace Turner could have seen her life ruined by her husband's desertion, as single mothers were treated much less kindly in the 1930s than they are today. Grace and Robbie Turner are recipients (and victims, ultimately) of the wealthy Tallises' social philanthropy. Grace Turner is an important part of the theme of social class and mobility that permeates *Atonement*.

(A03) KEY CONTEXT

Emily Tallis is suspicious of PC Vockins because he has been associated with 'carrying pamphlets' (p. 146) and being a member of a trade union (p. 146): trade unions regularly campaign to narrow the gap between the rich and the poor. Emily Tallis shows disdain for PC Vockins's wife, who talks about 'the price of chicken feed' (p. 146), which Emily believes is vulgar, and she is disappointed that PC Vockins does not show her the 'deference' (p. 146) she expects.

Key quotation: A missed opportunity **(A01)**

At one key point in the investigation, Briony is given a clear chance to escape from the action she has set in motion. She tells the policeman 'I know it was him', and the policeman replies 'Let's forget what you know' (p. 181). At this point, she goes on to confirm repeatedly that she is certain that she saw Robbie, even though this is not true. It is for this, and her later maintenance of this position, that she must spend the rest of the book atoning.

Revision task 5: McEwan's portrayal of the police **(A05)**

Make brief notes on the author's portrayal of the police officers. How does McEwan convey the following?

- Social class
- The language and behaviour typical of police officers

PART TWO: PAGES 191–201

Summary

- The **narrative** has switched to the perspective of Robbie Turner, now a soldier in war-torn France, and has moved on by five years to 1940. He is desperately making his way through the French countryside towards Dunkirk, where he has the best hope of escaping France to return to England.
- Robbie has been injured in the side but has not told his companions, Nettle and Mace, about his injury. Fever and pain make him absent-minded.
- They come across a bombed house and Robbie sees a child's severed leg in a tree. He has to go behind a wall to be sick. The soldiers continue on their way, Nettle and Mace teasing Robbie benignly about women. They pass through a swarm of bees, and Robbie's knowledge of rural life saves them from injury.
- They come across a farmhouse and ignore the protests of an elderly woman who tries to drive them away. She claims that her sons will kill the soldiers, but Robbie demands that they have food and water and shelter in a barn. She gives them a scant supply of poor food.
- Later in the evening, the woman's sons come to the barn. Robbie, Nettle and Mace assume they have come to kill them, and Robbie pulls out his gun, but the men are carrying baguettes, not weapons, and have brought good food and wine. All the men talk, Robbie acting as interpreter.
- The French brothers tell a sad tale of going to look for a cousin and her children in a bombed-out village, of finding corpses on the road, and of fearing the arrival of the German army. They finally leave the three to sleep.

Analysis

The road to Dunkirk

The contrast with the first part of the novel is stark. It is not clear for two pages that we are now sharing Robbie's point of view. In this way he is introduced anew, almost as though he is a different character.

The spectacle of the child's leg in the tree is shocking, to Robbie and to us. The flat, unemotional account of its fact lets the horror speak for itself. The description of the plane tree first, and then the leg, makes it clear this is a common scene in the war-torn landscape. The fact that Robbie is embarrassed by his disgust and his subsequent need to vomit is testament to how many horrors the men have witnessed – the others are able to disregard it and Robbie fears they will see it as weakness that he cannot. This leg is the 'unexpected detail' (p. 191) referred to at the start of the chapter, and stays with Robbie as a disturbing image that he struggles to get out of his mind.

The hostility of the old woman is initially comic, though dangerous in that it nearly leads to her sons later being shot by Robbie. We reflect differently on her behaviour on hearing that she had already lost a son in the First World War and that she has become confused by old age and grief. The brothers' account of their journey, and their disappointment and wonder that the German army is again in France, makes real the human impact of the war.

PART TWO: PAGES 202–13

Summary

- Unable to sleep, Robbie feels the wound in his side, which is throbbing uncomfortably, confirming his suspicion that it has a piece of shrapnel in it.
- He reflects sadly on the boy killed in his bed – the 'vanished boy' (p. 202) – on the thoughtlessness of the bombers, and then on his own lost youth wasted in prison. Robbie thinks about the possibility of being captured and spending the rest of the war in a prison camp, knowing he would not survive a second incarceration.
- Robbie recalls his last meeting with Cecilia and how her letters sustained him in prison. The two had become intimate in their letters, writing in code and referring to books they knew in order to bypass the censorship of the prison wardens.
- Their meeting for tea in London was awkward, but they shared a long kiss before Cecilia took her bus back to the hospital. Their plans to meet before Robbie was sent to France were thwarted by the early declaration of war.
- Robbie reads a letter from Cecilia in which she tells him of Briony's wish to meet up and Cecilia's hope that it might mean Briony wants to set the record straight and clear Robbie's name. This introduces the theme of Briony's atonement.

Analysis

A better life than prison

The combination of his earlier life and his time in prison has prepared Robbie well for the army and France, and explains the regard in which Nettle and Mace hold him, despite his inferior rank (Robbie could not apply to be an officer because of his criminal record). His accounts of the stifling oppression of prison – Robbie reflects that 'prison made him despise himself' (p. 206) – make the consequences of Briony's actions painfully real. His military training feels 'rich in variety' (pp. 207–8) in comparison and he thrives in the army.

A letter from Cecilia

Cecilia's final letter conveys her love for Robbie and her reaction to Briony's change of mind. Cecilia has grown up, and learnt to deal with trauma. She has spent years waiting for Robbie, 'feeding on the same memories that consumed him every night' (p. 205). Her nursing training and her rejection of her family have moulded her adult character.

Cecilia makes clear that she will never forgive the rest of her family, but admits her excitement at the news of Briony's possible retraction. She also displays empathy for her sister and her choice to become a nurse.

Key quotation: The process of war

(A01)

Although McEwan does not shy away from presenting the reader with the very real horror of war in this section, it could be argued that the most horrific aspect of the war is the 'indifference' (p. 202) that is shown to so much suffering. Robbie reflects that the war is an 'industrial process' (p. 202) in which the end product – death and terrible injury – is hardly considered.

(A03) KEY CONTEXT

Alfred Edward Housman (1859–1936) (p. 213) wrote *A Shropshire Lad* (1896), a collection of poems about love and nature, painting an idealised picture of the English countryside. Robbie mentions Housman several times; this could suggest a desire for the peace of the English countryside in the horrors of the war.

(A04) KEY CONNECTION

The lines 'In the nightmare of the dark, All the dogs of Europe bark' on page 203 are from the poem 'In Memory of W. B. Yeats', by W. H. Auden. The Irish poet and dramatist W. B. Yeats died in 1939; the lines refer to the hostilities and preparations for war all around Europe.

Summary
....

- After less than forty-five minutes' sleep, Robbie is woken by the corporals and they set off again across the fields.
- Robbie guides them, using the map-reading skills he developed in his youth. His companions' teasing irritates him, and he wants to be rid of them.
- Finally, they join a long line of vehicles, soldiers and civilians slowly retreating. Robbie hopes to lose the corporals, but when he becomes impatient with a civilian driver Mace and Nettle come to his rescue, preventing him from hitting the man.
- They pass a field in which a cavalry division is shooting its horses. Robbie's injury is becoming inflamed and walking is difficult.
- A major tries to pull Robbie from the line to join a futile attempt to attack some Germans he says are hiding in the woods, but Robbie is saved by a surprise attack on the column by a German plane.
- After the attack, Robbie helps move the wounded, and Mace and Nettle help to bury a boy before they continue on their way to Dunkirk.

Analysis
....

A long slow walk
....

This section evokes the weary, slow progress that the men make across the French landscape, the pace of the **narrative** echoing their trudging. They are stalled by the assault from the air, delayed by the major's attempt to recruit them to his ludicrous plan and held up further by their acts of kindness – helping the wounded, giving their last sips of water to an elderly woman, and burying the boy. We applaud their compassion and generosity, surprising and humbling after all that they have suffered. The nobility of their selfless actions is underlined by Robbie's determination to continue and the narrowing of his focus to just 'walking across the land until he came to the sea' (p. 219). The beat of the words echoes his footfall, and we feel every step of the long, terrible journey.

Repressed feelings
....

McEwan is careful to evoke the full horror of the war, here and later in the novel. The young boy they bury had a real life, demonstrated by the row of fountain pens in his pocket. He had a family and social context, represented by the distraught grandparents. Robbie's suppressed distress – 'Turner looked away, determined not to be drawn in' (p. 219) – at seeing the bodies of the women and children in a ditch makes us aware of the relentless barrage of horror he must face, and how he must still focus on his own survival.

A02

Study focus: The dark humour of war

When Robbie glimpses 'Mace's head on the grass by a pile of dirt' (p. 224), we, like him, fear it is no longer connected to Mace's body. There is macabre **comic relief** in realising he is only hidden, digging a grave. Many texts that deal with war use humour as a strategy for exploring the unrelenting horror, such as *Catch-22* (1961) by Joseph Heller. Look for other examples of humour in this section.

KEY CONTEXT **A03**

In retreat, the British army shot their horses and destroyed vehicles that they could not take back to Britain in order to prevent the German army from using them. Horses could not be evacuated by boat, nor left to wander the French countryside.

KEY CONTEXT **A03**

To be disobedient or rude to an officer could result in a charge of insubordination and severe disciplining. This is why Robbie is surprised by Nettle and Mace's behaviour towards the major (p. 221).

PART TWO: PAGES 226–34

Summary

- Much of this section returns the reader to the past in England. As Robbie marches, he revisits the sensual memories that have sustained him. He thinks again of Cecilia's last letter with the promise it holds that Briony may retract her statement and enable him to clear his name.
- Robbie wonders why Briony maintained so fervently that it was he who assaulted Lola. Robbie is also mistaken in his interpretation of events, convinced that Briony is doing this maliciously.
- The only reason he can think of is that when she was ten she had played a dangerous trick, pretending to drown, in order to see a demonstration of how much he cared for her. She then told him she loved him, and Robbie wonders if his rejection of her childish affections led her to harbour a grudge and plan her revenge.
- Briony later recalls this episode too (p. 342) but reveals that she had immediately forgotten about it after it happened.

Analysis

Thoughts of home

As Robbie recreates a summer day in England in his memory, it is a welcome relief from the marching and despair of the present, for us as well as for him. The idyllic picture of the pool 'below overhanging trees' (p. 230) in the woodland in summer, though rendered realistic by its dangerous currents and Briony's foolish act, is worlds away from the harsh realities of war-torn Normandy. There is a strange connection between the two, though, in the danger of death – then by drowning, now from war, and a few pages earlier from a swarm of bees – that is ever-present. The theme of the fragility of human existence is always close to the surface in this novel.

Progress booster: A dual structure (A02)

There is a **duality** to the structure of *Atonement*, with the past and the present, England and France, war time and peace time, humour and horror, truth and lies, and so on, often being presented side by side. Throughout the novel you should consider the way in which comparison and **juxtaposition** are used to explore themes and characters.

The mystery of other people's thoughts

It is a sad **irony** that, just as Briony misinterpreted Robbie's letter and embrace with Cecilia and found malice in them, so Robbie in his turn misinterprets Briony's testifying against him as 'infantile destructiveness' (p. 233). As he believes she deliberately lied in order to spite him, it is hardly surprising that he finds it impossible to forgive her. It is yet another facet of the novel's continuing exploration of how little a person can know of another's mind, how difficult it is to untangle actions and understand the motivation behind them or the connections between them.

(A05) KEY INTERPRETATION

Robbie considers, and we must agree, that the 'lasting damage' (p. 234) that has come to him as a result of the false conviction is that he cannot forgive Briony. He has even, while 'raging drunk on cognac' (p. 229), fantasised about killing her with his bayonet. He recognises that it is an ugly change in his character and, like the lost years, cannot be undone.

PART TWO: PAGES 234–46

Summary

- Returning to the walk to Dunkirk, Robbie sees a woman with her six-year-old son and tries to help her. At first, she follows his lead but eventually will only sit on the ground and hug her child. Robbie has to abandon her and run, but is thrown off his feet by a bomb blast that kills the woman and child.
- Parched and half-suffocated by the mud in his mouth, he makes his way into a wood. He sits there in a daze until Mace appears, bringing him water.
- When Robbie and the soldiers reach the bridge over the Bergues–Furnes canal they find that a sergeant is plucking soldiers from the rabble to work on holding the perimeter against the advancing German army.
- Robbie limps, supported on either side by Mace and Nettle, to avoid being picked out by the sergeant. They can see planes attacking the troops waiting on the beaches for evacuation, and the number of wounded and dead by the roadside increases.
- Nettle throws away his boots, but Robbie persuades him to take them back and carry them. He has already prevented the two corporals from throwing away their greatcoats – he knows they will be needed.

Analysis

Robbie's helplessness

As the relentless marching and stream of horrors continues, Robbie asks, 'What were they expected to do? Carry a dozen men on their backs when they could barely walk themselves?' (p. 245). It is true that he can do nothing to help, and there is so much suffering that any possible gesture would be lost in the enormity of the disaster. It is clear from his question that he feels guilty that he cannot help – he is defensive in proclaiming his impotence in the face of it all, and later he reflects on the extent of his own guilt (pp. 262–3).

Scenes of terror

The terrible scenes witnessed are thrown into relief and rendered yet more horrific by the fragments of everyday life glimpsed amongst them – the man ploughing and sheltering from the gunfire beneath a tree as though sheltering from rain (p. 235), the man and boys on the barge (p. 244) and, earlier, the woman and girl buying shoes (p. 216). Robbie is right that one day normal life will resume, but it is hard to believe in the midst of the chaos.

Study focus: A journey surrounded by death (A05)

'Each individual death is an explosion in itself, wrecking the lives of those nearest.' McEwan wrote these words of the 9/11 terrorist attacks, but he demonstrates the same idea in *Atonement*. He studied images from the conflict in Bosnia (1992–5) and drew on them in writing of the devastation in northern France. Robbie's mind is wandering as they finally make it into Dunkirk and he feels 'weirdly light-headed' (p. 245). The differing ways in which the soldiers react to the deaths of those around them in this section could be considered as McEwan's way of exploring the effect of war on our humanity and capacity for compassion.

KEY CONTEXT (A03)

André Maginot (1877–1932) was a French minister for war who gave his name to a defensive line of concrete bunkers built along France's border with Germany. The German invasion of 1940 attacked France by bypassing the Maginot Line (mentioned on page 234). By early June, Germany had cut off the Line, although some French commanders were keen to carry on defending it.

KEY CONTEXT (A03)

The incident on page 240 of the two men operating the Norton motorcycle, one working the pedals and the other steering, is drawn from McEwan's father's experiences during the Second World War – injured in the legs, he shared a Harley-Davidson with a comrade whose arms were injured.

PART TWO: PAGES 246-65

Summary

- Robbie drifts in and out of lucidity as exhaustion and the fever induced by his infected wound take their toll.
- On the beach they find a disorganised rabble of thousands, lolling about and standing in the sea waiting as a result of a 'chaotic retreat' (p. 247); there are no boats. Robbie and his two companions head for a bar, but there is nothing to drink.
- A group of soldiers begins intimidating a lone RAF man, blaming him for the failure of the RAF to support the army. Violence erupts, and Robbie realises there is little time before the assault on the man will become unstoppable. As he weighs up the possibilities, Mace rushes forwards and grabs the man. Nettle and Robbie help him escape.
- In a backstreet Robbie and Nettle ask an old woman for water. She demands that they first catch her pig and, though Nettle is reluctant, Robbie, in his delirium, is afraid she has power over his fate and agrees. In exchange she gives them good food and drink.
- The soldiers look for somewhere to eat and sleep. In a bombed hotel, men are dragging out mattresses, but a squabble starts and several fall downstairs. One man is left screaming with a broken back, while others step over him. Robbie and Nettle find a place in a crowded cellar and enjoy their meal in secret.
- As Robbie's fever worsens, his mind drifts between past and present. He wonders about the guilt and innocence of everyone involved in the war, and he plans to go back to the cottage where he saw the leg and bury the boy.
- Nettle wakes him because he is shouting, and tells him that the evacuation is in preparation. Robbie goes back to sleep and dreams of Cecilia telling him 'I'll wait for you. Come back' (p. 265).

Analysis

The absurdity of war

Robbie, Mace and Nettle have shown tremendous determination and courage in completing their terrible journey to Dunkirk. The first officer they meet, described significantly as popping up 'like a jack-in-a-box' (p. 246), does not see this and instead focuses on Nettle's untied shoelaces, calling him a 'disgrace' (p. 246). Turner is so disgusted by this, in his delirious state, that he considers shooting the officer.

Study focus: The significance of Dunkirk

A05

The gathering of thousands of British troops on the French beaches was the result of a catastrophic military defeat, but their eventual safe return was miraculous. When Robbie arrives he sees the apparently absurd hopelessness of the situation; thousands of men on the beach 'like grains of black sand' but only one upturned boat to be seen. Dunkirk could be seen as **symbolic** of both hope and **tragedy** – both important themes in *Atonement*.

A03 KEY CONTEXT

The troops' anger towards the RAF may surprise modern readers, however, many soldiers in the British army held the RAF responsible for heavy losses to German air raids. The RAF did not present an organised response to the Luftwaffe and, in 1940, had largely outmoded planes.

A04 KEY CONNECTION

Sebastian Faulks's war novel *Birdsong* (Hutchinson, 1993) presents a central character, Stephen Wraysford, who can be compared with Robbie Turner in his relationship with his fellow soldiers in times of great danger and distress. *Birdsong*, like *Atonement*, also moves in time between England in 1910 and in 1979 and so examines the effects of war on people and society across the twentieth century.

An outbreak of violence

The assault on the RAF man is horrific in its casual violence, its inevitability and its orchestration. The soldiers want to impress each other, to be applauded for their creativity in what they can think of doing to him. They are goaded by the man's helplessness – he is like 'a mole in bright light' (p. 252). The attack develops a deadly momentum resulting in a terrible sense of 'exhilaration' (p. 252).

Robbie is aware of the pattern it will take, having seen similar events in prison. He knows that he cannot simply step forward to speak out for the man as he will himself fall victim to the mob. He is too confused to formulate a plan, and even he is caught by the thrill of the moment, feeling 'unpleasantly excited' (p. 251). The episode is the more horrific and menacing because of the element of fun that is introduced into the account – the parallel with men enjoying a game of village cricket, the desire to maintain an elegant choreography with no discordant note.

Robbie suspects that if he spoke up the soldiers might be reminded of his humanity and brought to their senses. This seems a vain hope – the attack has its own dynamic and the people involved feel absolved of any individual responsibility.

Robbie's illness

Because Robbie's delirium is presented from his own point of view we, as readers, are left to infer that he is in fact not thinking clearly. For example, he appears to believe that a restaurant with 'a gramophone' and 'a wrought-iron balcony' (p. 259) is close by for their evening meal, even though all the buildings around Dunkirk are wrecked. Only the strangeness of these thoughts and Nettle's gentle disregard for Robbie's comments – 'get some sleep and no more of your ... shouting' (p. 264) – tell us that he is fevered. At the very end of the book, the older Briony reveals that (perhaps) he died in Dunkirk of blood poisoning, a condition that would have caused his delirium.

A senseless death

All the men have become so used to violence and death that the man with the broken back, who is left to scream 'almost inaudibly, as though in a panicky dream' (p. 258), is virtually ignored. Even Nettle and Robbie, who still have some compassion left, don't give him a second thought. Only we, as readers, will ever think of him again. He is a haunting reminder of the many senseless deaths of war, and a foretaste of the plight of the wounded that will be mercilessly scrutinised in Part Three.

Progress booster: Robbie's heroism

It is important for you to make links and comparisons across the text. Robbie has demonstrated considerable heroism and compassion in the course of Part Two, yet as he sinks further into illness and confusion he blames himself even for the death of the Flemish woman and her son who would not run from the air attack. It is a realistic evocation of how people in traumatic situations often feel responsible for things beyond their control, and contrasts with Briony's refusal of responsibility for her actions in Part One.

PART THREE: PAGES 269-77

Summary

- For this part of the novel, the **narrative** remains located in 1940 but has moved from France back to England where Briony is a trainee nurse in a London hospital.
- Briony's life is a round of menial tasks that she has to learn and repeat endlessly. She suffers under the stern authority of Sister Drummond and the strict regime of hard, physical work. Most of her time is spent cleaning.
- She is beset by apparently petty rules and regulations that, like army training, are designed to instil absolute, unquestioning obedience.
- Ominously, the wards are emptying and new supplies are turning up, including extra beds which have to be thoroughly cleaned.

Analysis

A life of rules

The regulations that seem petty to Briony recall some of the army activity we have glimpsed in Part Two. The stones painted white outside the hut on the perimeter of Dunkirk are a sign of one of the pointless tasks that occupy the army in less desperate times. In nursing, lining up the patients' noses with the creases in their sheets is a manifestation of the same mentality. Minor errors, such as 'walking back down the ward empty-handed' (p. 270), are considered worthy of severe punishment. The ward discipline, like the stone-painting, will give way to some degree in the coming onslaught. But the benefit of the training in unquestioning obedience will become clear, too, as Briony comes to rely on routine to carry her through the emotional trauma of dealing with war casualties.

Study focus: McEwan's use of literary devices

A02

Briony is not sure what to expect, but from the opening of this part of the novel it is clear that something is imminent. The swollen, turbulent river is **symbolic** of the state of the hospital and the whole city: McEwan uses **personification** to suggest how they both rise in 'unease' (p. 269). Something is growing, and soon it will burst upon them. There is a clue in the extra beds, which spread 'like deaths in the night' (p. 270), and the ominously large supplies of morphine, a powerful painkiller. A hapless probationer nurse is described **anthropomorphically** as having 'a cow's harmless gaze'. This provokes Sister Drummond's **metaphorical** 'lacerating' (p. 271) fury.

A04 **KEY CONNECTION**

Classic literature often presents vicious and terrifying scenes of violence to explore the darker side of humanity. Scenes from *Atonement* could be compared to the bloody death of Nancy in Charles Dickens's *Oliver Twist* (1839), the gang-related violence in Graham Greene's *Brighton Rock* (1938) and the multiple deaths in Shakespeare's *Hamlet* (1599) and other tragedies, for example.

Briony's developing style

Briony's writing style in this part of the novel is more assured and her new maturity is clear in her **narrative** voice, changed markedly since the first part of the novel. The self-consciously literary posturings of the very young writer have given way to poised and evocative prose, unhurried and confident. Long sentences that make use of the best – rather than superficially impressive – words make it a style that is easy to read and unobtrusive. We learn later (p. 277) that Briony writes an account of her days at the hospital in her notebooks, and presumably it is on these that the older Briony, as novelist, draws. The style captures the immediacy of the observed routine and experience with the eloquence of the older writer.

A new companion and a new life

Again, Briony finds herself thrown together with a girl of her own age, not of her own choosing. Her new companion, Fiona (who sleeps in the next bed), resembles Lola in having ginger hair and freckles, but is otherwise very different from Lola. The detail of her asking Briony to cut the fingernails on her right hand, a childish incompetence revealing her dependence on her mother, is in sharp contrast with Lola's attempts to be worldly and grown-up. Fiona is completely without guile, makes no attempt to pretend to be anything she is not and does not intimidate Briony in any way. 'Loud and jolly' (p. 273), Fiona is from Chelsea and her father is apparently a politician, so she has similar social standing to Briony. Briony finds in her a cheerful and unchallenging ally and she becomes her friend by default (p. 274).

The only clue that Briony may be disappointed with the change in her life – she has exchanged studying at Cambridge for working in the hospital – is in her reflection that she 'thought she was joining the war effort' (p. 275) but has ended up in the humiliating position of being commanded by Sister Drummond. This, though, is soon to change as her contribution to the war becomes very real.

Key quotation: A hint at Briony's continuing guilt — A01

Briony's new life is very different from the leisured privilege of her childhood, and the continuation of it that she had expected at Girton, following in Cecilia's footsteps. She expresses no resentment at the rigours of nursing, nor does she glorify the hardships to elevate her status as a martyr and penitent. In the first hint that she is paying the price for actions in the first part of the novel, she reveals only that she 'was delivered from introspection' (p. 276), the hard work and lack of time saving her from thinking about what she has done.

KEY CONTEXT — A03

The surname of one of Briony's fellow probationers, Susan Langland, is shared with medieval poet William Langland who spent much of his life reworking a single poem, *Piers Plowman*, which sought to show a way to salvation.

KEY CONNECTION — A04

For an entertaining and informative history of women and war, look at Kate Adie's book *Corsets to Camouflage* (Hodder & Stoughton, 2004). For a literary exploration of the pain of separation from a loved one, read *A Song (Absent from Thee)* by John Wilmot, Earl of Rochester (1647–80) or *Remember* by Christina Rossetti (1830–94).

PART THREE: PAGES 277–86

Summary

- In bed, Briony writes her journal, making up or embellishing some of the details.
- Briony's letters home are perfunctory and share none of her daily life. From her parents she hears that three families of evacuees have been sent to the house, and one of the evacuee children has broken the statue in the fountain. Local railings have been torn up to be melted down to make more planes for the war effort. Danny Hardman (the son of the Tallises' handyman, who is suspected of assaulting Lola by Cecilia and Robbie) has joined the navy.
- We learn that, before starting her training, Briony spent time living with an aunt and uncle in London and typed her first attempt at a story based around the events described in Part One of *Atonement*. She sent her story to a literary journal, *Horizon*, but has had no reply.
- She has also written to Cecilia – this is the letter discussed in Cecilia's letter to Robbie (pp. 211–13) – but as yet has had no reply from her sister either.
- Briony discovers that the British army is retreating to Dunkirk and realises that the preparations at the hospital are for the casualties from the defeat in France, and perhaps even from an imminent invasion of Britain. She tries to phone her father at his ministry, but is unable to get through to him.
- She receives a letter from her father telling her that Lola and Paul Marshall are to marry.

Analysis

Briony's feelings about home

Briony finds the other girls theatrical in their homesickness – the details in their letters are intended to 'astound their loving parents' (p. 277). This is **ironic** as overdramatising has been a feature of Briony's own character in the early part of *Atonement*. It highlights the changes in Briony herself and her determination to 'work for her independence' (p. 278). Another change is that she has gone from craving her mother's attention to withholding details of her new life from her parents. The letters from home make her feel nostalgic, but for us the concerns of her family look petty in contrast with the terrible events that Robbie has experienced and witnessed, and the horrific injuries that Briony will soon see. The literal destruction of parts of the family's country estate echoes the destruction of an era in English social history that the estate represents.

Briony: The developing writer

In Briony's account of her journal we glimpse the old Briony, still thinking she will become a great writer. She considers that 'she was really an important writer in disguise' (p. 280) – a childish turn of phrase that reminds us that she is still only eighteen in this section. Her thoughts about literature have changed, though. Now she hopes to be part of a new direction in English writing, one in which plot and character have given way to something else.

A03 **KEY CONTEXT**

Many types of food and some other goods were rationed during the Second World War. Each person was issued with a book of vouchers and had to hand over a voucher when buying restricted goods. It was not possible to buy more than the allowed ration in a week.

A03 **KEY CONTEXT**

The Nightingale School for Nurses in London was founded in 1860 by Florence Nightingale (1820–1910). It was the first nursing college in the world and marked the start of nursing as a trained profession. It was run on strict lines adapted from military discipline, as Florence Nightingale had developed her practices at Scutari during the Crimean War (1854–6).

Summary

- The nurses do not know why they have been given half the day off, but Briony and Fiona go to St James's Park to enjoy it. When they return to the hospital, the forecourt is crowded with injured soldiers, with more being unloaded from army vehicles.

- Briony and Fiona run across, just as staff come out from the hospital, and are drawn into work immediately. Briony feels inadequate as she struggles with the first tasks she is given, only partially succeeding at them. She takes one end of a stretcher, but can only just carry it to the ward and finally lets it slip. The jolt is painful for the wounded soldier and Briony feels she has failed.

- Her confidence increases as she deals successfully with several disturbing injuries including a young soldier who has had half of his head shot away and who dies in front of her. She finally feels better about herself when Sister Drummond compliments her on how well she has cleaned a soldier's wounded leg, removing several agonising fragments of shrapnel.

- Arriving at her room in the early hours of the morning, Briony finds a letter from the editor of *Horizon* refusing her story but with an encouraging commentary.

Analysis

From happiness to horror

This section has a cheerful, sunny start, with children playing outside 'on the grass shouting and laughing' (p. 288) and Fiona and Briony sharing 'cackles of hilarity and derision' (p. 289). McEwan, however, is leading up to a section that is unrelenting in its horror. We are suddenly plunged into a hellish nightmare of terrible suffering and horrific injuries. The first incident, nearly dropping the stretcher, is a shock to Briony and she is anxious that 'at the first moment of pressure, she had failed' (p. 292). Briony loses a troupe of men with crutches, and inappropriately tries to make soldiers get out of bed because she thinks she has to follow the right procedures. She is silently defensive when she realises the rules that have been drummed into her have been abandoned.

Progress booster: Comparing Robbie and Briony

A05

Both Robbie and Briony have had highly educated and privileged upbringings. Is it this that gives them the confidence to cope so well in such terrible circumstances? Once Briony gets into her stride, the 'brisk voice of the no-nonsense nurse' (p. 298) comes easily, and she is able to press on with terrifying procedures despite trembling and feeling sick just as Robbie is able to cope with the horror of France, despite his injuries.

The horror of war

The style of the writing does nothing to diminish the horror. There are several images drawn from familiar, domestic settings – the blackened leg like an 'overripe banana' (p. 296), the removal of blood-caked gauze likened to 'the famous tablecloth trick' (p. 296) Briony had seen at a birthday party, the plasma bags hanging like 'exotic fruits' (p. 295). The **juxtaposition** of the homely, comforting images with the men's agony throws the latter into sharp relief, making it all the more awful.

When Briony is sick in the sluice, it is mentioned as if in passing, with no emphasis and no hint of sympathy, making the point that this is nothing compared to what the men on the ward must endure.

McEwan's characterisation of the patients

Briony's last three patients have increasingly horrific injuries: each time we believe it cannot get any worse, and then find it does. The descriptions of the patients' reactions convey the terrible extent of what has happened to them, such as the desperate way in which Private Carter's eyes 'kept returning to the steel forceps' (p. 298). McEwan (or Briony) is keen to show us that these are real people, as we learn through the information we are given about their personality and background. They are not statistics and not like the illustrations in the clinical books which have been Briony's only previous exposure to the details of anatomy.

Briony's challenge

Briony adapts quickly. After the death of the French soldier, possibly the most devastating scene in the novel, she washes, changes her clothes and returns to work on the wards – though nothing she does afterwards warrants description. Even the senior, experienced nurses are out of their depth with the war wounded. Empathy cuts through the formality and orderliness which is still maintained. The accounts of the injuries are so graphic that the text becomes emotionally devastating to read and we, as readers, are also exhausted by the experience. Briony 'learned a simple, obvious thing she had always known, and everyone knew' (p. 304) – in this one night she comes to understand the sheer fragility of the human body in a way she could not begin to apprehend before.

A literary connection

The letter from Cyril Connolly addresses very different concerns and returns us to the Briony of the first part of the novel, the would-be writer. It is a curious passage, a detailed critique of a piece of writing we do not see but which has formed the basis of the early part of *Atonement*. Some phrases are still in the final novel; some details are different and the whole section describing the events round the fountain has been recast, following Connolly's suggestion, as a specific interlude in a larger piece with more **narrative** development. There is a more detailed account of this passage in the **Extract analysis** on pp. 48–9.

A03 KEY CONTEXT

McEwan has spoken about his vivid depictions of violence and its consequences: '[In writing about violence] you've got to embrace it, you've got to make your reader ... *see*. So, when people accuse me of being too graphic in my depictions of violence, my response is, "Well, either you *do* violence, or you sentimentalise it" ' (interview with Jonathan Noakes, in Margaret Reynolds and Jonathan Noakes, *Ian McEwan: The Child in Time, Enduring Love, Atonement* (Vintage, 2002), pp. 22–3).

A03 KEY CONNECTION

On page 314 Briony's story *Two Figures by a Fountain* is compared to the novel *Dusty Answer* by Rosamund Lehmann (1901–90), published in 1927. *Atonement* has echoes of its concerns and writing style. Lehmann's work explores the female consciousness in the interwar years.

KEY CONNECTION A04

Elizabeth Bowen (1899–1973) was an Anglo-Irish novelist and short-story writer. Her stories depict difficult relationships amongst the English upper middle classes – she could easily have been a model for Briony's writing. Love affairs with dark secrets are the subject of both the poems 'Porphyria's Lover' and 'My Last Duchess' (1842) by Robert Browning. A woman who loves a man accused of a terrible crime is a central theme of 'Peter Grimes' (1810) by George Crabbe (Cecilia has a collection by Crabbe in her flat, mentioned on page 335).

KEY CONNECTION A04

This letter is one of three significant letters given in their entirety and central to the plot. Robbie's letter to Cecilia in Part One and Cecilia's letter to Robbie in Part Two are the others. This recalls McEwan's interest in classic literature such as the work of Jane Austen and Charles Dickens, whose novels frequently feature letters.

EXTRACT ANALYSIS: PART THREE (P. 312)

Cyril Connolly's letter to Briony about the story she has submitted for publication comes before we know that Briony is the **narrator** of the entire novel. This extract from the letter is a serious literary critique of Briony's story. This is a kind of **metanarrative**, in which the writer – Ian McEwan – writes about his own writing.

Connolly's style has an informal tone with some personal engagement, but his language is studded with obscure words and turns of phrase, such as 'crystalline' (p. 312). He is comfortable with the **jargon** and process of literary criticism, saying 'and so on' (p. 312) after listing some erudite and complex point. He is careful, too, to acknowledge that the commentary is not all his own work. He uses a striking **metaphor** to indicate how Elizabeth Bowen's comments have been incorporated into, or 'mulched' (p. 314) into, his critique of Briony's work. The unusual use of the word 'mulched' (which usually refers to gardening) conveys his confidence in language, which could be seen to contrast with the strained and self-conscious writing of Briony. His measured style has a very polished surface, but hides

some cutting criticism. It resembles some of the novels of the day that presented emotional turmoil beneath a bland and disengaged relation of events. It is an accomplished evocation of the voice of an intellectual of the time.

Connolly appears to be aware that he is writing to a young person and he combines criticism with helpful and specialist literary advice. His first comment is that the story was 'arresting enough to read with dedicated attention' (p. 312). 'Arresting' means it caught his attention, and he is clear to Briony that this is an achievement in itself, commenting 'I do not say this lightly'. But he is, after all, rejecting the story. He goes on to point out some aspects that he liked before touching on his concerns about the piece. This is a formula often used in the professional world when giving feedback on an employee's performance, as it is encouraging to the person and makes them more receptive to the coming criticism.

Connolly uses a range of literary terms and references in his critique. His reference to the great **modernist** writer Virginia Woolf (see portrait, left) implies that Briony's writing is derivative, and that she has failed to develop a style of her own, but it can also be seen as a compliment for him even to mention Woolf in relation to Briony's story. The phrase 'attempts at characterisation' (p. 312) is patronising, saying that Briony has tried but failed to capture the characters. He uses the term 'crystalline present' to convey the way in which the descriptive writing of Virginia Woolf makes a crystal-clear picture of a moment captured in time, and it is clear that this is a writing style that Briony uses. However, Connolly says that it is better suited to poetry, that it presents 'stylised' thought processes and is useful for 'experimentation'. This suggests Briony is still learning and has sent him an experiment in composition. The implication is that the style is not likely to produce finished, mature works. Using the word 'vagaries' (p. 312), which means 'wanderings', makes it sound pointless and trivial. It appears that Connolly does not greatly like the 'unpredictability of the private self' (p. 312), a trait he shares with the younger Briony of Part One.

The image of 'the long grass stalked by the leonine yellow of high summer' (p. 312) – the nature imagery and difficult vocabulary make this a phrase written in the style of Virginia Woolf – conjures up a vision of a lion stalking through long grass, even though it means only the colour of a lion is present. It is so original and arresting that it is instantly recognisable from its use in Part One. This is the first clue that Briony wrote Part One (and indeed the whole of the novel) herself.

It could be argued that letter seems to disrupt the flow of the **narrative**, which up until this point has been very driven by plot and character. It is as if McEwan is presenting a criticism of the novel itself, drawing attention to the process of writing and to the artificiality of the whole idea; the novel we have is the product of drafting and redrafting, criticism and adaptation. This part of the novel could be described as **postmodern**, reflecting a movement in which writers and artists refer to themselves and their work within the work itself. The words from Connolly, which we are reading here, have supposedly shaped the way the book has finally turned out. Connolly's point that the work would be more engaging if there were 'an underlying pull of simple narrative' (p. 312) has been addressed in that the episode with the vase and Briony's observation of it does now lead somewhere. They also remind us of Briony's earlier thoughts that narrative and character were somehow old-fashioned in writing – here Connolly is reminding her, and the reader, of their crucial importance. This tale, like all of McEwan's fiction, has a huge narrative pull, driven by the terrible inevitability that emerges from people responding, in character, to tiny accidents and choices. Perhaps the final draft of *Atonement* is for McEwan a justification of his own decision as a writer to structure the text as he has.

PART THREE: PAGES 315–27

Summary

- After the initial chaos, the hospital routine slows down a little, and Briony works regular, thirteen-hour shifts. She becomes increasingly aware, however, of the expected, imminent invasion by the German army. This lends urgency to her plan to visit her sister.
- Briony feels vulnerable and clumsy as she makes her way across London with an ancient map. Despite her recent experiences, she is still immature in her relation to the world outside.
- Briony makes her way to the church where Paul and Lola are getting married and slips inside to watch. There are few guests in the modest church – only the immediate families of Lola and Paul. Although she wants to stand up and say that she knows a reason why they should not marry, she cannot find adequate words.
- She reveals to the reader that she now knows that Paul assaulted Lola, and that in their marriage the secret of it is locked away forever. Lola seems to recognise her and frown, but of the other guests only the twins know who she is. She allows them all to leave before she goes outside herself.

KEY CONTEXT **A03**

On the orders of the government, London street names and signs were painted over and maps were not available. The intention was to make it as difficult as possible for any invading troops to find their way around.

Analysis

A difficult journey across London

Although Briony has been exposed to much in the hospital, outside she is anxious. The strict routine and rule of the hospital have robbed her of any confidence in acting for herself. The threat of an impending invasion, as well as the rumours that German spies are now dressing like 'nurses and nuns' (p. 318) in order to go undetected, makes her paranoid, 'inept' and 'unnerved' (p. 319).

Paul and Lola's marriage: A terrible sham?

This is the first time we learn that Briony has decided that Paul committed the assault. Until this point, we may have believed that the scratches and bruises Lola revealed to Briony in her bedroom were inflicted by the twins. The revelation that it was Paul Marshall is shocking, as is the fact that Lola is about to 'marry her rapist' (p. 324). This marriage hides a dark secret, as they have both colluded in Robbie's false imprisonment. Furthermore, there is no suggestion that the only true lovers, Cecilia and Robbie, may marry.

Key quotation: London during the war **A01**

McEwan/Briony describes wartime London as aggressive and frightening. For example, a train is described as a 'brutal invention' that 'belonged to a race of supermen' (p. 320). This gives a sense of the alienation and dehumanising effects of war, similar to the transformation of the French countryside that Robbie observes in Part Two.

Revision task 6: Separations and divorces **A05**

There are no positive depictions of marriage in the novel. Emily and Jack share a hollow partnership and Emily's sister Hermione is in the process of divorce in Part One, for example. Make brief notes on the separations and divorces in *Atonement*.

PART THREE: PAGES 328–49

Summary

- Briony is on her way to see her sister, though we do not immediately know where she is heading. Reluctant to get there too quickly, she stops for breakfast in an unpleasant café 'with smeared windows, and cigarette butts all over the floor' (p. 329).
- When Briony arrives at Cecilia's home, she encounters a hostile landlady, a 'tall, sharp-faced woman' (p. 330), and a no less hostile Cecilia.
- Cecilia has little interest in Briony's news from home, except for the information that Betty has broken Uncle Clem's vase. It is clear that the rim Cecilia mended broke away while Betty was carrying it, and Betty was unjustly blamed for the accident which in fact resulted from Cecilia's actions – a tiny parallel to Briony's own guilt.
- When Robbie discovers that Briony is there, he is 'angry, very angry' (p. 340) and can barely contain himself. Briony sees Cecilia calm him with the 'tenderness' (p. 343) that she used to calm Briony as a child. There is still misunderstanding, as Briony does not know that Cecilia and Robbie, in their own misinterpretation of events, have blamed Danny Hardman for the assault and built up an unfounded hatred towards him.
- They are shocked to learn that Paul was the rapist, and that Paul and Lola have married; 'Wedding? This morning? Clapham?' (p. 347).
- Robbie instructs Briony to swear an oath, write him an explanation and tell her parents the true version of events. He and Cecilia then escort Briony to the underground station so that they can spend their last hour together before Robbie rejoins his regiment.
- Briony anticipates writing her new account, which will be her atonement for her error.

Analysis

A conclusion

This is both the end of the main part of the novel and its beginning, as Briony determines to write a new version of the story, 'an atonement' (p. 349), which will eventually become the novel we have just read. The signature, 'BT / London 1999' (p. 349), is the first indication that the whole book has been written by Briony in old age. This realisation inevitably colours our appreciation of all that has gone before, demanding that we re-evaluate our reading of the novel immediately.

A final encounter with Cecilia and Robbie

Cecilia and Robbie have both changed. Made sterner by passing time and their terrible experiences, they have lost the excitement and optimism of early adulthood. They are no longer embarking on an exciting journey, but surviving a gruelling life. The hazy, languid days of Part One are a long way off – there is a sense that the early part of the novel was unreal but that now everyone, including Briony, has grown up and this is what existence really is. The love between Robbie and Cecilia is an adult, sustaining love. The fierce urgency of passion they displayed in the library is recalled in the harsh physicality with which Cecilia draws Robbie back from the brink of violence, when they seem 'like wrestlers' (p. 343) to the alarmed Briony.

(A03) KEY CONTEXT

The phrase 'Lady Muck' (p. 334) means a woman with social pretensions. McEwan, in his essay 'Mother Tongue' (*The Guardian*, 13 October 2001), recalls how his mother jokingly referred to herself as Lady Muck once. It is possible that it is included as a tribute to her.

(A03) KEY CONTEXT

The wallpaper, striped 'like a boy's pyjamas' (p. 335), recalls the leg and scraps of pyjama fabric at the start of Part Two, and their bar-like pattern which 'heightened the sense of confinement' recalls Robbie's time in prison. Both are shadowy reminders of Robbie before he comes into the room.

Progress booster: Characterisation

A05

Briony's experiences as a nurse have given her enough insight to know that she will never be able to see what Robbie has seen, feel as he feels – and yet, in writing her story, she has shown us his experiences and feelings. This can be seen as a comment on the right and obligation of the novelist to delve into the psyche of characters they have created, but at the same time recognises that ultimately each person is knowable only to him- or herself. Fiction requires that the writer is able to imagine as fully as possible what it is like to be someone else, and helps the reader to do the same. Through *Atonement*, McEwan may be suggesting that empathy is the key to understanding and describing other people's actions and, as such, to being a good novelist, and it is something that Briony painfully acquires.

KEY INTERPRETATION **A05**

McEwan has said 'It is hard to be cruel once you permit yourself to enter the mind of your victim. Imagining what it is like to be someone other than yourself is at the core of our humanity' ('Only Love and Then Oblivion', *The Guardian*, 15 September 2001). This idea of compassion and empathy illuminates Briony's later motivations and character.

The continuing theme of truth and memory

It is **ironic** that Robbie and Cecilia have also clung to an inaccurate version of the events in 1935. Their certainty that Danny Hardman was guilty, with no more evidence than Briony had for believing Robbie to be guilty, parallels Briony's misunderstandings and false beliefs. It is only a combination of circumstances that has turned Briony's mistaken belief into a catastrophe, while Robbie and Cecilia's mistaken belief has no significant consequences at all.

An ambiguous ending

The chapter concludes on a hopeful note. Briony, in her 'serene' (p. 349) state of mind, is still holding on to her naive belief that she can make things better in some way, and Cecilia and Robbie are happy together. This is all to be undermined in the **epilogue** as we learn that there is no simple **resolution** to the novel, and that, in actual fact, this reconciliation between Briony and Cecilia is only in Briony's imagination.

Key quotation: Briony's hopes

A01

In comparison to the worldly and cynical Robbie and Cecilia, there is still something of the naive child in Briony. She keeps hoping for some reconciliation, forgiveness or even a sign that this will be possible in the future, and desperately imagines she could regain her 'post of beloved younger sister' (p. 329). The word 'post' could suggest a 'role', as if being a 'nurse', a 'sister' and so on are all somehow dramatic parts that Briony inhabits.

'LONDON, 1999': PAGES 353–71

Summary

- The elderly Briony is tidying her papers at the end of her last retelling of her tale, which has become *Atonement*. She has vascular dementia, a degenerative brain condition that will lead to the loss of memory and then all other faculties and functions until she dies in a few years' time.

- On the morning of her seventy-seventh birthday, Briony goes to the Imperial War Museum Library to deposit some letters from Robbie's fellow soldier in France, Nettle.

- As she arrives, she sees Paul and Lola leaving, but avoids meeting them. Paul is old and frail; Lola is sprightly. Briony reflects on their charity over the years, wondering whether they have been trying to atone for their own crime.

- Briony realises that, as Lola will outlive her, it will be impossible for her to publish her novel in her own lifetime.

- A minicab collects Briony to take her to her childhood home, now converted to a hotel. Pierrot has organised a performance by the assembled children of Briony's **melodrama**, *The Trials of Arabella*, which they watch in the library.

- Alone in her room, Briony reflects on how she has represented history, and makes the stunning revelation that, although she has redrafted *Atonement* many times, this is the first time she has allowed the lovers to survive until the end of the book. She suggests that, in fact, Robbie died in France and Cecilia in the Blitz.

Analysis

The 'real' story of Robbie and Cecilia?

The epilogue is remarkable in unpicking all that has gone before. The contract that we have entered into with the novelist, to believe in the events narrated, is now void. The story is at an end, and Briony steps back to tell us how much was true, and to stun us with her rewriting of the ending. In saying that she can see no virtue in presenting the bleak 'true' end of Robbie and Cecilia's history she is returning to her earlier position of wanting a balanced and satisfying story, one 'sealed off at both ends so it resembled … every other finished story in the world' (p. 6). Briony, of course, has not now done this, as the epilogue undermines her plan.

The reversal raises the questions of what a reader wants and expects from a novel, what the novelist is under an obligation to deliver and whether the **narrator** has any duty to truth. The complex issues of memory and truth, woven throughout the novel, are given another unexpected twist by the news that Briony is losing her mind and that soon all will be lost beyond recall. (There is more about this in **Themes: Writing and imagination** and **Themes: Truth and memory**.)

A03 **KEY CONTEXT**

The account McEwan gives on pp. 354–5 is not particularly characteristic of either vascular dementia or Alzheimer's disease, but the reader needs to be clear that Briony is slowly losing control of her mind and her memories. Her diagnosis could be seen to add a final subtle layer of doubt as to whether Briony is communicating with full clarity and accuracy, adding to the ambiguity of the **narrative**.

A03 **KEY CONTEXT**

McEwan has referred to Leo Tolstoy's (1828–1910) 'crucial question' as being relevant to Briony's concern that all is lost in death: 'My question – that which at the age of fifty brought me to the verge of suicide – was the simplest of questions, lying in the soul of every man … Is there any meaning in my life that the inevitable death awaiting me does not destroy?' (*A Confession*, Part V).

Key quotation: Aging characters

A01

We see many of the characters from the first part of the novel ravaged by age. It is an unpleasant shock to see Leon in his wheelchair, 'curled and slumped to one side' (p. 365), paralysed by a stroke. Paul Marshall appears 'somewhat reduced' (p. 357), and Briony is on the brink of degeneration. Lola is fiercely defiant of old age, 'as lean and fit as a racing dog' (p. 358) with a slightly frightening energy that is perhaps born of decades of protecting and denying the secret at the heart of her marriage.

The Tallis house sixty years later

The Tallis house is changed, but Briony is barely nostalgic for it, having already renounced it as her home long ago. Its new name, Tilney's, takes us back to the passage from *Northanger Abbey* before the beginning of the novel which quotes the down-to-earth Henry Tilney berating the overly imaginative Catherine Morland. The once romantic, classical family home has now become a functional business and is **symbolic** of the decline of the upper classes after the war.

KEY CONTEXT **A03**

Shakespeare sometimes allows an authority figure to step out of the fiction at the end of a play and draw attention to the fact that it was all play-acting, all made up. This happens in *The Tempest*, *A Midsummer Night's Dream* and *Twelfth Night*, for example.

Progress booster: Alternative histories

A02

The glimpses of other characters' histories – Leon's marriages and the early death of his first wife, the deaths of Jackson and Emily, Briony's own marriage to a Frenchman, her father's second marriage – all hint at other stories that could have been told. But, just as we might be believing in this final, outer, fiction, Briony/McEwan undermines it again with the suggestion that she could rewrite even the **epilogue** and put Robbie and Cecilia in the library watching the play. We end with the sense that we do not know what is real; we can never know 'what *really* happened' (p. 371). In stepping back, Briony prompts us to reflect that perhaps the whole story was all made up after all. When analysing this novel it is helpful to step outside it, to see how it is constructed and to assess the role that the theme of writing and rewriting plays.

....

PROGRESS CHECK
....

....
Section One: Check your understanding
....

These tasks will help you to evaluate your knowledge and skills level in this particular area.

1. Is Briony a reliable **narrator**? List two reasons for and two against this.

2. Write a paragraph outlining your understanding of the marriage of Emily and Jack Tallis.

3. List three instances of violent behaviour in Part One of *Atonement* and comment briefly on their significance.

4. Make brief notes on Lola, Pierrot and Jackson's attitude towards their parents' divorce.

5. Find three details that suggest Paul Marshall is portrayed as an unpleasant character even before the rape of Lola.

6. Write a paragraph on the setting of the Tallises' house and how its changes through the book reflect the decline of the upper-class lifestyle of the 1930s.

7. Find three examples of the way in which Mace and Nettle depend on Robbie for their survival.

8. What is the significance of the child's leg in the tree? Find two or three instances where Robbie is reminded of it and explain what it represents to him.

9. In what way are works of literature used in *Atonement*? Find three times when literary texts are referred to and explain what they reveal about character or theme in *Atonement*.

10. Speculation and incorrect assumptions are themes underpinning *Atonement*. Life during the Second World War was also characterised by misinformation and unfounded fears. Find three examples where Briony is described as fearing events in wartime London that we know never came to pass.

11. What does the encounter with the dying soldier Luc Cornet reveal about Briony's character as a young nurse? Write a paragraph using quotes to support your response.

12. What significance do meals and food play in *Atonement*? Pick three examples and rank them from most to least significant.

13. Is Emily Tallis a **sympathetic** character? Give two reasons for and two reasons against.

14. Make brief notes on the role of Danny Hardman in the novel.

15. List some of the ways in which the false accusation of Robbie has affected Cecilia's life.

16. Make a list of some of the military slang and specialist words that Robbie and the other soldiers use in Part Two and their meaning. For example 'cavalry' (p. 219) = soldiers who ride horses.

17. Briony's challenging work as a nurse is part of her atonement. Find three or four details that illustrate the tough regime that Briony works under as a trainee nurse in London.

18. Make brief notes on the significance and symbolism of Uncle Clem's vase.

19. What is the significance of Briony's childhood play, *The Trials of Arabella*? Make two points about its significance in Part One and two points about its significance in the final section, 'London, 1999'.

20. Find three examples of where water is significant in the novel.

Section Two: Working towards the exam

Below are five tasks which require longer, more developed answers. In each case, read the question carefully, select the key areas you need to address, and plan an essay of six to seven points. Write a first draft, giving yourself an hour to do so. Make sure you include supporting evidence for each point, including quotations.

1. Explore the role of nature and the natural environment in *Atonement*.
2. In Part Two we learn that Briony has written the novel as an act of atonement. How does this affect the reader's response to events and descriptions?
3. Consider the role of misunderstanding in the novel.
4. How does the novel depict the changing role of women in the twentieth century?
5. Ian McEwan's novels are often described as macabre or horrific. What role does the macabre play in *Atonement*?

Progress check (rate your understanding on a level of 1 – low, to 5 – high)	1	2	3	4	5
The significance of particular events and how they relate to each other					
How the major and minor characters contribute to the action					
How McEwan uses the device of changing points of view					
How McEwan structures the novel					
The final outcome of the story and how this affects our view of the protagonists					

CHARACTERS

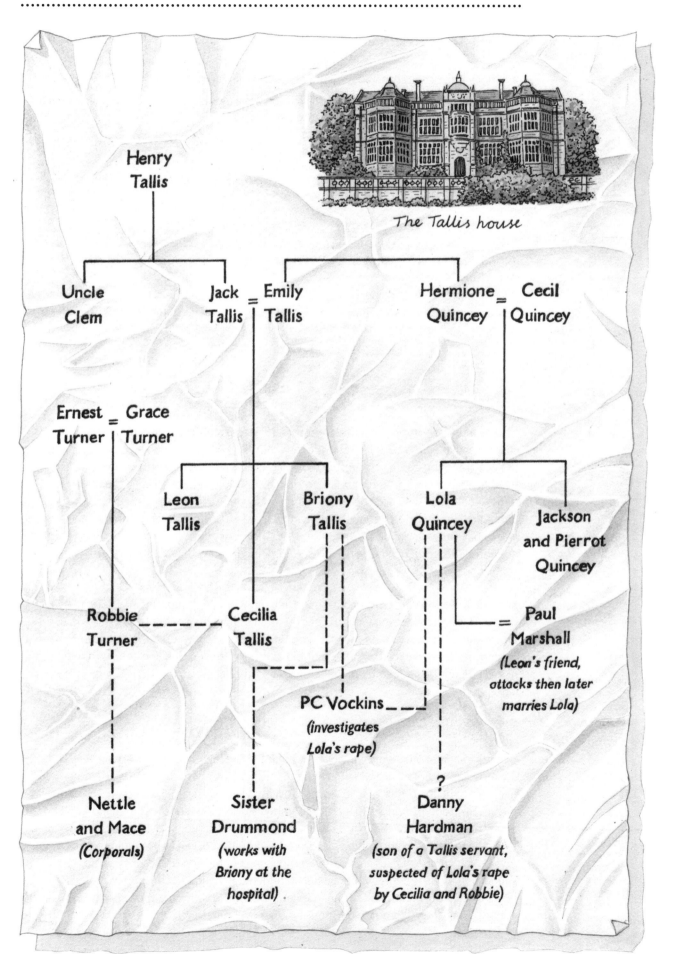

The Tallis house

Henry Tallis

Uncle Clem

Jack Tallis = Emily Tallis

Hermione Quincey = Cecil Quincey

Ernest Turner = Grace Turner

Leon Tallis

Briony Tallis

Lola Quincey

Jackson and Pierrot Quincey

Robbie Turner _ _ _ _ Cecilia Tallis

Paul Marshall
(Leon's friend, attacks then later marries Lola)

PC Vockins
(investigates Lola's rape)

Nettle and Mace
(Corporals)

Sister Drummond
(works with Briony at the hospital)

?

Danny Hardman
(son of a Tallis servant, suspected of Lola's rape by Cecilia and Robbie)

Briony Tallis

Who is Briony Tallis?

● Briony is the central character of the novel and the main **narrator**.

● She appears at three stages of her life: as a thirteen-year-old girl, as a young woman of eighteen and as an elderly woman of seventy-seven.

● Briony is finally revealed to be the writer of *Atonement*.

A life of privilege

The young Briony has been largely neglected by her parents but has otherwise had a privileged early life. She likes to see herself as a writer, and is desperate for drama. Her family has indulged her literary attempts. Everything she sees or does becomes potential material for her stories, making her somewhat callous in relation to other people and their experiences. She wants to be the centre of attention, and has little concern for the feelings or desires of others. Briony's own verdict on her younger self (and so presumably what she is aiming to convey in her portrayal of herself) is that she was a 'busy, priggish, conceited little girl' (p. 367), though this is certainly not the whole picture.

The end of childhood

In Part One, Briony is poised on the brink of adolescence, and is beginning to shun overly childish activities and demonstrations of affection. The dangerous mixture of a child's view of the world and the desire to be respected by adults and thought worthy of participating in their realm leads to disaster: 'At this stage in her life Briony inhabited an ill-defined transitional space between the nursery and adult worlds which she crossed and recrossed unpredictably' (p. 141). The young Briony may seem precocious and educated, but she can also behave as 'an indignant little girl' (p. 141). She judges herself as being 'childish' (p. 35) for not bothering to change her dirty dress, comparing herself unfavourably to the sophistication of the young Lola.

Briony's obsession with writing goes hand in hand with her thoughtlessness. She marshals her cousins into rehearsing with no consideration of how they might feel. She is equally inconsiderate in abandoning the play when she decides to give up drama, believing that her writing 'had been defaced with the scribble of other minds' (p. 36), and concentrate on the new direction she has identified for her fiction – fictional prose.

A devastating accusation

Briony's imagination rapidly convinces her that Robbie is Lola's attacker. Briony labels him as a 'maniac' (p. 119) – a word which the young Briony clearly has little understanding of – and her need to be the centre of attention is satisfied by being the only witness to the crime. She pushes her doubts aside, certain that she 'knows' Robbie did it because it fulfils her wish for a satisfying, tidy **narrative** in which events are played out as they should be. She finds a villain who acts true to form and can be discovered and punished, just as he would have been in one of her own moral tales, and so 'the terrible present fulfilled the recent past' (p. 168). Any suggestion that she might withdraw her statement or change her position is met with hostility from the adults, and her need for approval and attention is then enough to make her adhere to her story and quash any doubts in her own mind.

KEY CONTEXT **A03**

'When I got to the end of *Atonement* I felt that Briony was the most complete person I'd ever conjured' (Ian McEwan, interview with Jonathan Noakes, in Margaret Reynolds and Jonathan Noakes, *Ian McEwan: The Child in Time, Enduring Love, Atonement* (Vintage, 2002), p. 23).

Study focus: Briony the writer

From the very start of the novel, Briony's passion for writing is key to her personality, and to the development of the plot. McEwan withholds the information that Briony is the writer of the book, forcing the reader to re-evaluate the narrative once this has been revealed.

Briony is childishly callous in ransacking experience for her fictions. In imagining she might find the twins floating face down in the swimming pool, 'She thought how she might describe it' (p. 156). Most importantly, she sacrifices Robbie to her desire for a fulfilling narrative, making him the protagonist in the rape with no consideration for the impact it will have on him and others when she has doubts about his guilt. Her lack of empathy at this point limits her writing as well as making her unthinking in her treatment of other people. When she matures, she is able to imagine being someone else – she is quite right to say it was growing up that changed her mind (p. 342). The change to being able to empathise with others brings guilt as well as creative success. As a nurse, her writing becomes 'the only place she could be free' (p. 280), with writing being presented as a kind of therapeutic and healing act.

A04 KEY CONNECTION

Michael Frayn's novel *Spies* (2002), also set during the Second World War, tells how two young boys, inspired by the atmosphere of suspicion at the time, allow their imaginations to run wild, with dire consequences for the adults involved. Like *Atonement*, it reflects on the problems faced by children in negotiating adult worlds.

Briony the nurse

Five years later, the Briony of Part Three has grown up enough to realise what a terrible thing she has done. She is admirably brave in her **resolution** to do something about it, but as a young adult she is still unsure and immature in many of her actions. During the course of Part Three, Briony is forced to grow up more. She knows it is 'necessary to stay away' (p. 279) from her family while she undergoes her self-inflicted punishment and gains her 'independence' (p. 278). The arrival of the horribly injured men at the hospital brings her face to face with real suffering and death. Not all her childishness is stripped away, though: she is naive in her hope that Cecilia and Robbie can forgive her – 'she had never thought of herself as a liar' (p. 336) – and that she can make everything all right in some way. She also has childish fantasies about being thought a spy as she makes her way across London, running 'nursery rhymes' (p. 319) through her mind.

Dementia approaches

We know little of Briony's life in the period between Part Three and the **epilogue**, 'London, 1999', increasing the sense that her crime has been her life's key event, and her atonement its main focus and driving force. She has been a successful novelist, she has married a French man (reminding us of Luc Cornet and his mistaken declaration of love). She is wealthy, living in central London, taking expensive taxi rides and wearing 'cashmere' dresses (p. 361). Her extended family shows affection and makes an effort to celebrate her birthday and her life, so she is clearly popular amongst them. In the face of dementia, she is not yet panicking, commenting 'it might turn out to be somewhat benign' (p. 354) as she imagines a peaceful, unaware death.

At the very end of the novel, Briony is passing out of the other side of adulthood. We see her always on the boundaries – of adolescence, of adulthood and now of death. These are times for reflection and re-evaluation, and times when past actions are seen in a new light, although she still feels 'something heavy' (p. 358) on her heart when she catches sight of the Marshalls. She knows there can be no going back over her work again and so has completed her final draft of the book and atoned as far as she is able, saying 'My fifty-nine-year assignment is over' (p. 369).

A02 KEY QUOTATION

'How can a novelist achieve atonement when, with her absolute power of deciding outcomes, she is also God?' (p. 371).

Has Briony achieved atonement? McEwan invites the reader to consider the role of the **omniscient narrator** in constructing character and event; Briony admits that she is able to tell this story in any way she choses. The assignment of the female gender to God is also an interesting **postmodern** choice, in which the old certainties of beliefs, traditions and structures are constantly questioned.

Robbie Turner

Who is Robbie Turner?

- Robbie is the son of Betty Turner, the Tallises' maid, but he is treated as a member of the Tallis family.
- Robbie is in love with Cecilia Tallis but is wrongly accused by Briony Tallis of raping Lola Quincey.
- After his prison sentence, Robbie serves as a soldier in France in the Second World War. It is suggested that he dies from an infected wound there.

A university graduate

In Part One, Robbie is fresh from studying English at Cambridge and has his whole life spread out before him, thanks to the 'liberation' (p. 86) of his education. Because he enjoys the patronage of Jack Tallis, he has the luxury of being able to change his mind about his future career. After a degree in English, he first plans a career in landscape gardening and then turns to medicine, which requires expensive retraining. Is he flighty and indecisive, or multitalented and unable to choose how to channel his energies for the best? It is hard to tell: the range of opportunities available to him emphasises how much is lost in the closing off of his life and in his early death. His talent and determination to work hard are unquestioned, and he is already studying alone to prepare himself for medical training.

A man of many skills

Robbie is decisive and active, attributes that are demonstrated in the way he writes to Cecilia when he recognises his feelings for her, and goes to dinner with the intention of confronting her. He teaches himself medical terminology, reads 'landscape books' and quotes Freud (p. 84). His intelligence and adaptability stand him in good stead in France, where decisive action and determination to take charge of his own destiny are essential to survival. In smaller details, too, he is prepared for France. He speaks French (p. 199), and his skill at map-reading and his passion for walking make it possible for him to navigate a route to Dunkirk.

A good man, falsely accused

Robbie's abilities, his physique, his intellectual prowess, his ease in company and with himself all make him attractive. He has always been generous and caring with Briony – the story of her swimming lessons and his response to her stupid action in throwing herself into the water (p. 232) demonstrate this. In France, too, he is generous and selfless and deeply traumatised by witnessing the death of a young mother and son who are 'vaporised' (p. 239) by a German bomb. He and his companions are compassionate in their treatment of the bereaved grandparents and the victimised RAF man.

Robbie comes across as a genuinely good person, making it all the more terrible that he is imprisoned for a rape he did not commit. The only hints of callousness in his behaviour in France are when he feels himself drawn to the unfolding spectacle of the RAF man's beating, which makes him 'unpleasantly excited' (p. 251), and that he, like everyone else, walks on past the cries of the injured in the ambulances after the Stuka attack. In London, he has to suppress his aggression towards Briony and wants to kill Paul Marshall: 'He ... was fighting off an emotion he did not want witnessed' (p. 343). These lapses are sufficient to keep him from unbelievable saintliness, but insufficient to taint him.

Robbie's anger

At the end of the meeting with Briony in Part Three, Robbie is able to suggest a way forwards, a path that could help her atone. It costs him immense effort, but he is able to contain his anger: 'His eyes were steady, and he had everything under control. But there were drops of sweat on his forehead' (p. 345). The older Briony also allows herself to have Robbie acknowledge a glimmer of understanding of her mistake. When Briony says that she saw a man Paul's height he says 'My height' (p. 346). It is both a warning against being certain again and a recognition of how an error can begin.

Study focus: Robbie and the theme of love

The main focus of Robbie's character is his love for Cecilia and his determination to survive for her sake – 'she was his reason for life, and why he must survive' (p. 209). Her love and his hope for a future with her sustain him through prison and in France. It is a powerfully felt erotic love as well as a deep romantic love. His extended recollection of their love-making in the library makes this clear: 'the ... memories that consumed him every night' (p. 205). The intensity of feeling conveyed in it is sufficient to convince us of his love and desire for her enduring through the ensuing events.

Love and the urge to survive form the driving principles of Robbie's character in Part Two. But he has other attributes. His love for literature and art, born out in his eloquent language and graphic descriptions which have the quality of painting in words, fill out his personality. Like Briony, he has enthusiasms – in his case, art, literature, gardening, walking, medicine. These make real his potential to live to the full, and so increase the agony of his life being wasted in the barren environment of prison. Unlike Briony, Robbie is fully able to engage and empathise with others of any social standing, a compassionate man who is deeply embedded in the social fabric.

Progress booster: A character to identify with

Notice how Robbie is the character given most introspection. We are party to his private thoughts more than to those of any other character. The younger Briony is handled with **irony**, which creates distance, and makes her character less likeable. Robbie is genuinely likeable, and we are given such unlimited access to his inner state that we **identify** and empathise strongly with him. This is necessary not just for Robbie to be a credible character but for the full impact of his wrecked life to be felt – this would fulfil Briony's aim to achieve atonement through her empathetic portrayal of the man whose life she has ruined.

Key quotation: Robbie Turner

In Parts Two and Three, Robbie is shown as a mature man. Though sobered and made more cynical by his experiences in prison and in the army, he is fundamentally as honourable, generous, compassionate and fair a person as ever. The anger that could have poisoned his character is focused sharply on Briony and the people who supported her story – it has not made him generally embittered, nor wrecked his personality. Robbie knows 'he would never forgive her' (p. 234).

A05 KEY INTERPRETATION

Robbie's frustration leads him to go out into the night to search alone for the twins. In another glimpse forward, we are told that he would reflect many times that this seemingly slight choice 'transformed his life' (p. 144). The crisis of the novel has been set in motion.

A04 KEY CONNECTION

Compare Robbie Turner to Fortinbras from Shakespeare's *Hamlet* – both are active and compassionate soldiers who are seen as a contrast to the troubled and problematic characters who surround them.

Cecilia Tallis

Who is Cecilia Tallis?

- The older sister of the Tallis family, at the start of the book Cecilia has just finished a degree at Cambridge University.
- Cecilia falls in love with Robbie, who is falsely accused of raping Lola by Briony.
- Abandoning the Tallis family, Cecilia trains as a nurse in London.

Life after university

After coming home from Cambridge, Cecilia has spent the summer at the family house, but is frustrated at her inactivity. She had expected everyone would be pleased to see her and keen to involve her in things, but in reality the time has been empty. She has decided to spend time in the family home not because she wants to but because of 'a vague notion that her family was owed an uninterrupted stretch of her company' (p. 20). This leads her to sacrifice her time to them, a gesture that she petulantly acknowledges they do not appreciate.

A desire for attention

Like Briony, Cecilia has a childish desire to be the centre of attention. She puts herself at the heart of domestic matters, imagining herself to be indispensable to the smooth running of the household. However, we know that she has been away during term time for three consecutive years, and, despite Emily's ineffectual management, the house has not lurched from one crisis to another. She has an exaggerated sense of her own practical importance – 'She simply liked to feel that she was prevented from leaving, that she was needed' (pp. 21–2). She is in awe of Leon and will not stand up to her father, while her mother does not value her intellect. She is a realistic product of the low regard in which girls were sometimes held at the time.

At the start of the novel, Cecilia is also something of a snob. She assumes that it is social difference, and his desire to highlight it, that led Robbie to remove his shoes and socks before entering the house earlier in the week. We learn later from Robbie that it was out of concern for Polly who was cleaning the floor, and because he feared his socks were smelly. Consideration, not social awkwardness, motivated his gesture. Cecilia has overinterpreted his action, imbuing it with more significance than it has. Robbie's revelation of the mundane and generous reality reduces Cecilia in our eyes, making her look laughably priggish.

Progress booster: Comparing two sisters **A01**

Consider the parallels and contrasts between Briony and Cecilia Tallis. In Cecilia's liking for dramatic gesture we can see her family resemblance to Briony. She is concerned about how she looks to others. It is Cecilia's determination to project an image, as having the good taste to present flowers with a 'natural ... look' (p. 23), that leads to the accident with the vase. She looks at her own current experience as though she is reflecting on it from some point in the future. When she opens the obscene letter from Robbie, she 'adopt[s] an expression of amused curiosity' (p. 111). Like Briony, too, she forms ideas precipitately which she then sticks to with determination. She decides that Danny Hardman is guilty, with no more evidence than Briony had for deciding Robbie was guilty of the assault. Likewise, Cecilia infers that Robbie is conscious of his social inferiority and interprets his behaviour in this light. She believes that he is punishing her 'for being in a different circle at Cambridge, for not having a charlady for a mother' (p. 27), and that this is the cause of the awkwardness between them.

A theatrical streak

Cecilia is not as theatrical as Briony, but her concern with how she appears to others is related to her tendency to pick a role and then play it. In Part One, she sees herself playing the part of a sophisticated young woman of her era, recently down from Cambridge and bored with life in the country. She is anxious talking to her brother, presenting her news in the way she thinks best suited to the impression she wants to create. During the night of the crisis, she adopts a dramatic, tragic pose, setting herself apart, chain smoking and wringing a handkerchief. She stares at her family, 'unable to believe her association with such people' (p. 179).

The adult Cecilia

The Cecilia of Part Three bears little resemblance to the awkward, slightly snobbish and self-important young woman of Part One. She has suffered – by being separated from Robbie and alienated from her parents, despising her once-loved sister and living the tough life of a wartime nurse. Briony comments that there 'was a hardness in her tone' (p. 332) with eyes 'enlarged, by fatigue perhaps. Or sorrow' (p. 332). Her only enthusiasm appears to be negative – to distance herself from her family and cut herself off from her former life and character. Her singularity of purpose is not unrealistic – it is typical of people who become passionately devoted to a cause or campaign – but it makes her a less appealing character to us.

A03 **KEY CONTEXT**

Vera Brittain's *Testament of Youth* (1933) gives an autobiographical account of nursing in the First World War.

A fierce love

While Robbie has the whole of Part Two in which to project his character, Cecilia has a more shadowy presence, filtered through the letters that she writes to Robbie. This increases the sense that she is an innocent bystander rather than a main player. She is fierce in her love for, and defence of, Robbie, saying in her letters he is 'my reason for life' (p. 209). She is a successful nurse but there is nothing now of her love of literature, other than a few books in her down-at-heels room (p. 335), and no mention of any other source of joy in her life. Cecilia's 'new' character perhaps suffers from being a projection of the older Briony's desire to mould her to her own purpose. Cecilia is passionately in love with Robbie still. Her devotion to him and certainty of his innocence have led to her isolation and she chills Briony when she casually states 'I won't ever forgive you' (p. 337).

Study focus: The 'real' Briony?

It is important to remember the two possible endings to Cecilia's life – that she was killed in 1940 and Briony 'never saw them in that year' (p. 370). One interpretation is that the older Briony created the adult sister she would have liked to have had. It is notable that none of the younger Cecilia's faults (being overdramatic, obsessed with appearance and petulant) is in evidence in Part Three. Perhaps writing her a near-perfect character for posterity is part of Briony's atonement.

Key quotation: Cecilia **A01**

'Lovers and their happy ends have been on my mind all night long' (p. 370).

The reader has to bear in mind that Briony has created the version of Cecilia presented in *Atonement*. This fact can open up alternative interpretations of the descriptions of Cecilia as Briony attempts to achieve her atonement. Is this portrait of Cecilia 'reliable'?

Lola Quincey

Who is Lola?

- Lola is the eldest of the three Quincey siblings – her mother is Emily Tallis's sister.
- Lola is attacked and raped by Paul Marshall at the Tallis house when she is fifteen years old.
- Later she marries Paul and becomes the successful Lady Marshall.

A precocious child

Lola is keen to appear more grown-up than she is. She dresses in as adult a manner as she can, and she uses **idioms** and behaviour copied from her mother in dealing with the twins. She resembles a caricature of an angry mother, grabbing Jackson's ear and using **clichéd** phrases such as 'How *dare* you say that' and 'You will never *ever* use that word again' (p. 57). She acts the grown-up, too, in chastising Paul Marshall for saying that he had read about her parents in the papers. She is patiently indulgent of Briony's **melodrama**, though she cunningly manages to take the lead role for herself. At the same time, she is still very much a child. She relishes the chocolate bar, and knows how annoying it must be for the twins that she has it and they do not. She joins in Briony's excited condemnation of Robbie's letter, and it is she who comes up with the word 'maniac' (p. 119) to describe him.

KEY INTERPRETATION A05

Lola's name is an abbreviated form of Lolita, the central character of the novel of the same name by Vladimir Nabokov (1955). Twelve-year-old Lolita – or 'Lola' – is the focus of the central character's sexual obsession. In choosing the name, McEwan may be suggesting that she is becoming aware of her own sexuality, certainly of her attractiveness. A film version of *Lolita* came out in 1962, directed by Stanley Kubrick.

Study focus: Lola – the willing victim A02

It is never clear whether Lola might actually be a willing partner in the action with Paul Marshall. Briony's words at Lola's wedding suggest she may have been:

> Poor vain and vulnerable Lola ... who longed to throw off the last restraints of childhood, who saved herself from humiliation by falling in love, or persuading herself she had ... And what luck that was ... to marry her rapist. (p. 324)

Even if she were willing, her young age means that Paul's act would still be criminal. The nature of Lola's own crime, though, would be different (and possibly worse). The evidence is ambiguous. Emily Tallis hears a stifled sound which she thinks is Paul and Lola, and both of them come to dinner with injuries. Paul has only a slight scratch, while Lola has extensive bruising and scratches which suggest that she was restrained. Lola makes no attempt to avoid Paul and is not obviously upset when Briony first finds her. She had made one breathy cry before Briony knew she was there and is not crying; what Emily heard in the nursery was a squeal of laughter – neither is particularly alarming.

A shocking marriage

Lola's marriage to Paul in Part Three comes as a shock both to Briony and to the reader; the description of the wedding as something horrific, and as 'mausoleum' of truth (p. 325), is ultimately told from Briony's point of view, however, and may be biased. As Briony admits, 'Nor did the bride appear to be a victim, and she had her parents' consent' (p. 325). Lola may have conveniently fallen in love with her rapist to avoid humiliation and difficulties. Maybe she imagined herself in love with him from the start, or was so hungry for attention in the midst of her own domestic turmoil that she welcomed his attention. In any case, Robbie is as much a victim of Lola and Paul as he is of Briony.

An unfair judgement

We see some events through Lola's eyes before the assault, but judge her most from how Briony and Emily Tallis view her. Emily is resentful of Lola and sees in her many of the aspects of her own sister, Hermione, whom she dislikes. Her unfair view is that Lola is attention-seeking, demanding, prone to drama and selfish, and, like her mother, guilty of 'relentless preening' (p. 147). Emily believes that Lola is 'bound by an iron principle of self-love' (p. 147) with the harshness of the word 'iron' suggesting that Lola will never change. However, we do not see Lola demanding much attention. She is quiet during the dinner, says little about the assault, keeps her injuries hidden from the adults and takes part in Briony's play without complaint. She tries to impress Briony with her maturity, but does not impose herself on anyone else. She is, if anything, overly compliant and so easy prey for Paul Marshall.

'My high-living, chain-smoking cousin'

In old age, though, Lola is vigorous and robust, chic, steely and unassailable – 'a touch of the stage villain' (p. 358) in Briony's words – although even Briony admits she is 'an unreliable witness' (p. 358) in her comments on Lola's appearance. Briony is certain that, even if Paul dies, Lola will pursue a court case against her if she publishes her book revealing their secret. She has formidable energy and a 'terrible agility' (p. 358) which Briony senses comes from a deep sense of purpose, that of hiding her guilt and Paul's guilt. The rape, if rape it was, is part of a crime in which she colludes as well as being a victim. Lola and Paul are famed for their charitable patronage of many causes. There is a suggestion that this may be their way of atoning for what they have done, but Briony appears to give them limited credit for their generosity.

Key quotation: Lola   **A01**

On page 358, Briony comments that Lola could have been 'Cruellla de Vil' – a cartoon villain. Is this Briony making a hint that she is not entirely able to judge Lola dispassionately, because she still holds Lola responsible for Robbie Turner's imprisonment? This strikes an unusually humorous tone, possibly at Briony's own expense.

A04   **KEY CONNECTION**

In *A Passage to India*, by E. M. Forster, the white girl Adela Quested makes a false accusation of attempted rape against the Indian character Dr Aziz. There are interesting parallels with *Atonement*. Adela suffers a traumatic experience of some kind while visiting caves, and Aziz, as an Indian, is less likely to be believed than Adela – just as Robbie is less likely to be believed than Lola.

Paul Marshall

Who is Paul Marshall?

- Introduced to the Tallis family by Leon Tallis, Paul is a successful businessman who is making his fortune with the Amo chocolate bar.
- Paul Marshall attacks and rapes fifteen-year-old Lola Quincey (for which Robbie Turner is wrongfully convicted).
- Paul goes on to a long and successful life, marrying Lola and becoming Lord Marshall.

Arrogant and conceited

Paul Marshall is an unpleasant character from the time we first see him, but many characters in the novel do not recognise his failings. He has a grandiose view of what he does, describing how he has been 'for every waking minute of every day, enslaved to a vision' (p. 49). He appears quite ridiculous when it emerges that he has been managing the manufacture of the multicoloured Amo chocolate bar.

A need to be in control

Paul Marshall does not give the others at the Tallis house much chance to talk, delivering a monologue about himself. He imposes his own will without regard for good manners; the revolting cocktail that he forces on the party opens Chapter Eleven – 'melted chocolate, egg yolk, coconut milk, rum, gin, crushed banana and icing sugar' (p. 125) – and is inappropriately rich for a hot summer evening. If he touches Cecilia on the arm as they leave the terrace ('Or it may have been a leaf', p. 54), which seems likely, this is another example of him imposing on others. Of course, he does this most forcefully in his assaults on Lola.

Paul is impolite and overbearing in other episodes, delivering a 'ten-minute monologue' (p. 49) at one point. During the dinner, he speaks first to Robbie, leaning across Cecilia to do so. Robbie winces at the rudeness of Paul starting a private conversation before talk is properly under way. His ostentatious gesture of tipping Hardman five pounds is vulgar and inappropriate as we feel sure he is not motivated by generosity. Though Paul is of a higher social class than Robbie, he has fewer social graces and is 'conventionally dull' (p. 47). Paul is several times described as almost handsome, but his chin is too large and his features crowded towards the top of his face. He seems to consider himself handsome, however. It does not take Cecilia long to realise his limitations as she thinks how it might be to marry someone 'so nearly handsome, so hugely rich, so unfathomably stupid' (p. 50).

A sinister presence

The most ominous aspect of Paul's character is his unpleasant sexuality. His erotic dream about his young sisters and the lascivious way in which he watches Lola eat the Amo bar – '"Bite it", he said softly' (p. 62) – prepare the way for his attacks on her. He is bold, certainly, to leave marks on her which will be visible at dinner and this suggests that he either considers he is above suspicion or does not see anything wrong in his actions – he is used to taking whatever he wants. When Briony comes upon Paul and Lola on the island, he does not run off, but skirts around the clearing before disappearing. He acts calmly, too, during the aftermath of the assault back at the house, offering the police officers cigarettes (p. 175).

KEY CONTEXT A03

A total of over 53 million people died in the Second World War and the social structure of many countries across Europe and around the world was changed forever; this is reflected in the experiences of the Tallis family.

KEY CONTEXT A03

The value of a £5 note in 1935 was nearly forty times its current value, so Paul Marshall has given Hardman a tip of around £200 ($350 or €290) – a ridiculous amount.

Progress booster: Guilty on many levels

A02

It is important that you can write about the consequences of Marshall's crime. Paul's crime is not just sex with or rape of a minor, bad enough in itself, but allowing the innocent Robbie to be imprisoned for the assault. We are given no later insight into Paul's mind, and can guess at how he feels only from the few details of his later history that Briony gives us in Part Three and the **epilogue**. He marries Lola: this is a certain way of keeping his crime secret, and closes off 'what *really* happened' (p. 371) to everyone else: 'the truth ... was steadily being walled up within the mausoleum of their marriage' (p. 325). The marriage ceremony is uncharacteristically quiet and discreet. It is unlikely that this is just because of wartime shortages and austerity (they do have a Rolls Royce). It suggests that the marriage is a bit of an embarrassment, more an exercise in damage limitation than an expression of true love, at least for Paul.

A long and successful life

In 'London, 1999', we discover that Paul and Lola have lived very public lives, often in the newspapers, defending themselves enthusiastically against any possible libel. Briony wonders if 'he's spent a lifetime making amends' (p. 357). They have made charitable donations to various causes. They live in fear of discovery and may feel guilty about what they have done to Robbie, though Briony does not openly reflect on this. Paul, 'shrunk' and 'reduced' (p. 357), leans heavily on Lola; the image suggests that she now has the upper hand, that her response to the rape has been to hold him to ransom for the rest of his life.

Ironically, though Paul is morally undeserving of the social advantage he enjoys, he is ennobled, becoming Lord Marshall by the end of his life. It is a wry comment on the class system that a manipulative bully rises into the upper class through exploiting the commercial opportunity of the war, and that a rapist thus enjoys universal respect and admiration.

A04 **KEY CONNECTION**

'The Ruined Maiden' (1866) by Thomas Hardy draws uneasy connections between love, marriage, money and social morals just as the marriage between Lola and Paul does.

Key quotation: Paul Marshall

A01

Paul Marshall is a self-important character who appears to see the approaching war purely in terms of what he can gain. The narration takes an ironic tone as it echoes Marshall's own words and misguided thoughts: 'exhausted as he was, and maligned, he would not be turned away from his purpose, his vision' (p. 50).

Emily Tallis

Who is Emily Tallis?

- Emily Tallis is married to Jack and is the mother of Briony, Leon and Cecilia.
- Her marriage is lonely due to Jack's affair and work in London.
- She suffers from migraines and frequently withdraws herself from family life.

Emily Tallis's view of the world

Emily is characterised by selfishness and inertia and is noticeably absent from the first five chapters of the book. Cecilia often steps in when Briony needs comfort. Emily uses her proneness to migraine, labelling her actions as 'retreating before its threat' (p. 63). She has an image of herself at the centre of the house and 'gauge[s] the state of the household by straining to listen' (p. 65), but she does not actually engage with the household. Instead, she comes across as self-indulgent. She is trapped in her room, in semi-darkness, unable to live life to the full – but it is largely through her own choice. Her torpor – 'Emily lay back against the pillows for another several minutes' (p. 70) – extends to all areas of her life. She will not confront Jack about his affair and feels that they should not interfere in Robbie's life by paying for and encouraging his education – it 'smacked of meddling to her' (p. 151).

A romanticised view of motherhood

Emily Tallis would like to have another child and is already nostalgic for Briony's childhood. But it is her own lost position and eloquence that she mourns: 'she never spoke so well as she had to her eleven-year-old last-born' (p. 68). She enjoyed the feeling of easily exercised power that being the mother of a young child gave her, folding her daughter with arms trapped in 'babyish helplessness' (p. 68), and of being of central importance to someone with no physical, emotional or intellectual effort. Now she resents rather than values Briony's growing independence and considers her daughter's talent a demon (p. 68). Her own view of life is jaded and she is dismissive of the idea that 'the weary, self-evident world could be re-invented by a child' (p. 68).

Study focus: Arguments with the cook A02

Notice how Emily's arguments with the cook may seem a small detail but are revealing of her personality. Although Emily likes to think of herself as a controlling presence, she is in reality completely ineffectual. She is not able to manage the domestic staff. She makes an inappropriate choice of meal for a hot day and is unable to back down. Betty the cook's 'irritation [is] directed at Mrs Tallis' (p. 104) and it falls to Cecilia to find a solution to the problem.

KEY CONTEXT A03

'While the house succeeds in communicating that the Tallises are of high-rank ..., its lack of traditional, dignified elegance indicates to the reader ... that the family's concern is not status, but holding off history.' Ian Karamarkovich's essay 'The Tallis House as an Extension of Emily Tallis in McEwan's *Atonement*' (2015) explores the way in which the Tallis house shows the Tallis family's need for safety and privacy as much as their social class and wealth.

KEY CONNECTION A03

Another text that deals with a marriage that has grown distant, like that of Jack and Emily Tallis, is the poem 'One Flesh' by Elizabeth Jennings (1926–2001).

Progress booster: A life dictated by social class

Make sure you have an awareness of how Emily's views are traditional and bound by both her class and the age in which she lives. She is conservative and superficial, seeing no point in Cecilia studying and believing that it will make her unmarriageable. Unlike Briony and Robbie, for example, she sees no value in knowledge that is not of practical use. She passively accepts her ignorance, claiming 'Some things were simply so' (p. 149). She is snobbish, believing that it is not necessary for the family to be concerned with Robbie and his education, and seizes upon his supposed crime as evidence that she was right. Robbie comments later that she 'pursued his prosecution with a strange ferocity' (p. 227). For her to do anything with conviction is unusual.

An opportunity to break free

Contrastingly, in the moment of crisis in Part One, Emily rises to the occasion and takes charge. Cecilia is not capable of acting or willing to act, yet Emily 'actually grew as her older daughter shrank into private misery' (p. 175). It seems that Emily's seclusion and status as an invalid suited the whole family and that they colluded in allowing her to preserve her inertia. When something else is needed of her – and events seem to endorse her view of the world – she is able to break free of her habitual role, and apparently sustain it, if Robbie's account of her zeal is to be trusted.

Key quotation: Emily Tallis

Emily's children are accustomed to her uselessness and to humouring her: 'Whenever Mrs Tallis exercised authority in the absence of her husband, the children felt obliged to protect her from seeming ineffectual' (pp. 127–8). Emily does not volunteer to either look for the twins or phone the police as she does not grasp the gravity of the situation, seeing it instead as an extension of her sister Hermione's behaviour which she has so resented, and as significant mainly in being awkward for her. She assumes that everything and everyone is focused on her and is incapable of seeing any importance in events beyond their impact on her personally.

AO3 KEY CONTEXT

Scientific knowledge is an important element of *Atonement* and a number of other books by Ian McEwan, and he clearly does not share Emily's view that having a detailed knowledge of the world is not always necessary. A debate about whether scientific knowledge was the antithesis of artistic appreciation of the world emerged in the nineteenth century, but Briony and Robbie are both characters who appreciate academic and abstract knowledge as well as practical skills.

Leon Tallis

Who is Leon Tallis?

● Leon is Cecilia and Briony's older brother.
● He works in a bank but lives for pleasure and fun.

'The agreeable nullity of Leon's life'

Leon does not play a large part in the novel and, as we are not given any of the story from his point of view, he is presented only through other people. In the first part of the novel, Leon is filtered through Cecilia's adoration, the brother and sister being described as 'inseparable' (p. 67) at one point. Even so, the life she admires comes across as superficial and perhaps not as exciting as she imagines, and actually contains a great deal of 'blandness' (p. 108). He works in a bank, and spends his time rowing and seeing friends. He is 'somewhat relieved' (p. 108) not to be promoted, and all the events he describes have happened to other people, not himself. The impression is of an easy-going man with no ambition or goals.

A friend to Paul Marshall

Leon is undiscerning in his choice of friend: Paul Marshall is unpleasant and pompous, as well as being Lola's attacker. According to Leon everyone is a 'good egg' or a 'decent sort' (p. 107). It seems that Cecilia is in awe of Leon because of their childhood relationship and because he is her older brother, rather than for any particular character traits or achievements.

Key quotation: Leon | A01

Although Leon is 'soft and charming in company' (p. 109), covering for his mother's social awkwardness, he takes charge in speaking to his father when the twins disappear. In the **epilogue** we learn that he nursed a sick wife and brought up his children after her death, revealing latent abilities not apparent in Part One. The name Leon means 'lion', suggesting strength and stability. Cecilia feels comforted by his arm that has 'the consistency of tropical hardwood' (p. 110).

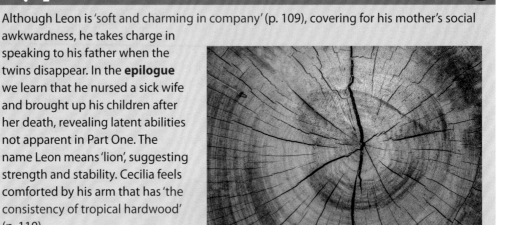

Revision task 7: Brothers and sisters | A02

Brother and sister relationships are explored in both *Hamlet* and Charles Dickens's *Hard Times*. Make notes on the Tallis and Quincey siblings' relationships in *Atonement*.

Nettle and Mace

Who are Nettle and Mace?

- Nettle and Mace are two British soldiers who walk with Robbie to Dunkirk.
- They look after Robbie as he succumbs to blood poisoning and delirium.
- In the epilogue, Briony has letters from Nettle, who has helped her to piece together the journey to Dunkirk.

Two Cockney corporals

As the two Cockney corporals with whom Robbie walks to Dunkirk are seen only from Robbie's point of view they have a tendency to blur into one. Nettle is the smaller, with a rodent-like face and protruding teeth. Mace is large and imposing. The two men exasperate Robbie, though in fact they have their uses and are good men.

Saving Robbie Turner

Robbie feels responsible for the corporals, but as soon as they join the main line of men marching to Dunkirk he thinks he has done all he is obliged to do and can lose them. He is wrong, however. Robbie needs their protection as much as they need his. His map-reading and navigation have been essential in crossing the countryside towards Dunkirk, but the corporals help and even save Robbie on several occasions. As Robbie's wound becomes infected, his mind wanders and his strength ebbs away. He depends increasingly on Nettle and Mace, with Nettle waking him to give him wine (p. 260) and to stop him calling out in his sleep (p. 263).

Brothers in arms

At the start of Part Two, Nettle and Mace annoy Robbie by teasing him about 'crumpet' (women) (p. 193), asking 'What's a private soldier like you doing talking like a toff?' (p. 193) and referring to him as 'her' (p. 215). They seem more hardened to the horrors of the war than Robbie is, since he dodges behind a wall to be sick after seeing the leg in a tree and it does not appear to affect them. But they are generous men. After a Stuka attack, they all stop to help the wounded.

Key quotation: 'That ain't the enemy, Guv'nor' **A01**

Nettle and Mace are more streetwise and shrewd than Robbie, and almost appear like guides in this hostile environment. They realise that Robbie looks likely to be pulled aside to man the perimeter defence outside Dunkirk and Nettle tells him to limp between them. They stop Robbie attacking the French civilian driver who annoys him, saying gently 'That ain't the enemy, Guv'nor' (p. 217), and they know to give the French farm brothers cigarettes, something that had not occurred to Robbie. Their trust in him, however, is based on their admiration for his intelligence and natural leadership.

A03 KEY CONTEXT

Nettle and Mace are the names of minor irritants: nettle is a stinging plant, and Mace is a brand of pepper spray used for personal self-defence (Mace was invented in 1970 but McEwan would be aware of its connotations for his twenty-first-century readership).

A04 KEY CONNECTION

Robbie's relationship with Nettle and Mace has echoes of Hamlet's friendship with Rosentcrantz and Guildenstern in *Hamlet* (1599), with its petty annoyances and jokes alongside a genuine sense of caring for one another.

THEMES

Atonement and guilt

An act of atonement

There are two crimes at the centre of *Atonement*: the attack on Lola, and Briony's false accusation. The accusation appears to have more far-reaching and devastating consequences than the rape itself. The rape is arguably a shadowy event, never clearly seen or investigated. Its consequences for Lola and Paul are barely explored other than in Briony's reactions to their shocking marriage.

Briony's writing of the novel again and again is her act of atonement for her crime. The false accusation wrecks the lives of Robbie and Cecilia, and for this Briony faces a lifetime of guilt. But how culpable is she? In her defence are her youth, her innocent (though foolish) motives and the lack of real opportunity she had to change or retract her evidence once adults had begun to act on her original statement.

Who exactly is guilty?

Briony is not the only person who is guilty. Most obviously, Paul Marshall is guilty. Lola is guilty, too, in remaining silent about who attacked her. Lola finds in Briony's certainty a chance to escape the humiliation and difficulty of accusing Paul (or accounting for herself, if she was a willing partner). Paul and Lola let Robbie bear the punishment for Paul's crime and are more culpable than Briony – she at least believes he is guilty while they know he is not. It is possible that Paul and Lola try to atone through their acts of charity, but theirs is a different story, not the one which Briony is intent on telling.

Perhaps it can be argued that Briony's family, the police and other experts involved in the prosecution should bear some of the guilt. Should her family have been able to recognise that her love of drama and her need to be the centre of attention made it very difficult for her to relinquish the position she had won by her certainty? Yet Briony cannot be absolved of all responsibility. When given the clearest chance, early on, to change her evidence, she refuses it: 'Yes, I saw him' (p. 181) she says when the police officer tells her to disregard what she knows and think only of what she saw: ' "You saw him with your own eyes." "Yes, I saw him. I saw him" ' (p. 181).

Progress booster: Guilt

Make sure you can write about how guilt extends through the novel, in the war, to the whole of society. At the end of Part Two Robbie, the most guiltless of characters, reflects on his own guilt. The Second World War was the most destructive event in human history. The span of the novel has seen 'First his own life ruined, then everybody else's' (p. 217). No one remains innocent:

> What was guilt these days? It was cheap. Everyone was guilty, and no one was ... there weren't enough people ... to take down the statements of all the witnesses and gather in the facts. The witnesses were guilty too. (p. 261)

Social responsibility

Robbie feels guilty for the people he has not saved, the dead he has not buried, even though he realises that he could not save everyone. This does not mean guilt is not there, just that it is diffused. Everyone is guilty, by sins of omission if not of commission, of the war and its destruction of individual lives and society as a whole. It is a stark message of social responsibility, as relevant at the time when McEwan was writing as when Robbie is speaking. The fragile peace in Europe, patched together after the First World War, has been shattered. Guilt extends backwards in time, as well as forwards. When Betty is blamed for breaking Uncle Clem's vase, we know it was not her fault. It, too, had been pieced together inexpertly.

Key quotation: Atonement and guilt **A01**

It is worth remembering that McEwan portrays many small acts of guilt that are built into the larger picture of the novel; this may be staying silent or not acting. Emily is guilty of neglecting Briony and of neither searching for the twins nor calling the police; Lola is guilty of keeping silent; Cecilia is guilty of hiding her breaking of the vase; Robbie is almost guilty of doing nothing to save the RAF man, but is saved from this crime by Mace – an important act of redemption. (Indeed, Robbie is set apart from this general trend of guilt through inactivity by his tendency to decisive action.) The message extends to all of society, then and now: 'You killed no one today? But how many did you leave to die?' (p. 261).

War

On the brink of change

The Second World War is a presence throughout the novel even though it is most immediate and important in Parts Two and Three. In Part One, the war is impending and casts its shadow over the action. It makes itself felt in the Tallis household through Jack's war work and Paul Marshall's hopes to cash in on any conflict by selling a camouflage version of Amo bars: 'the Army Amo' (p. 62). It crops up, too, in casual references to Hitler and to the Abyssinian Crisis, creating a background awareness that casts an ominous shadow over the easy, pleasant lives of the Tallises.

Emily dismisses Jack's statistics that predict 'five million casualties' (p. 149) as improbably pessimistic, and the twins repeat to Paul their father's opinion that 'there isn't going to be a war' (p. 62), but as readers we are aware of the war as historical fact. The life depicted in Part One is fragile, and the sense we have of its imminent destruction adds to its strange, elusive quality.

Progress booster: The ongoing presence of the First World War **A03**

Make sure you can write about the influence and effects of the First World War on the **narrative**. This can also be seen in the disappearance of Robbie's father, whom Grace likes to think died in the war rather than simply ran off, and in the changed social hierarchy which has meant that Robbie and Cecilia have both been to Cambridge. The First World War reappears in the battlefields of northern France in Part Two, with the old woman who has lost a son 'near Verdun in 1915' (p. 200) and the French farmers bewildered at the return of the German army. Thus we see lasting effects of the previous war even as the Second World War is just starting.

A03 KEY CONTEXT

McEwan has written and spoken extensively on politics and responsibility, including articles on the 9/11 attacks and the terrorist bombings in London in 2005 (see 'Only Love and Then Oblivion', *The Guardian*, 15 September 2001; and 'How Could We Have Forgotten that This Was Always Going to Happen?', *The Guardian*, 8 July 2005).

A03 KEY CONTEXT

The Second World War saw far fewer British casualties than Jack's department anticipated. There were 62,000 civilian deaths and 326,000 soldiers killed but Britain was not invaded. France suffered similar military casualties, but 470,000 civilian deaths. In Germany nearly 4 million civilians died.

Everyday torments

The experiences of Robbie, Nettle, Mace and the people they encounter span a range from discomfort to agony. McEwan neither glorifies war nor ignores the more mundane suffering that was the lot of the majority of participants. Robbie and his fellow soldiers are disabled by blisters and bleeding feet (Nettle at one point refuses to wear his boots, which are causing agony, p. 245), by exhaustion, hunger, thirst and aching wounds.

These experiences are not glamorous – they are the everyday torments often overlooked in depicting soldiers' lives but which make up the bulk of wartime experience. There are terrible bursts of violence – 'a hand whipped out and slapped the man's face' (p. 251) – casually committed atrocities and transgressions against human decency, but the constant grind of marching and searching for food, drink and somewhere to sleep make up the major part of the soldiers' day. McEwan tells us 'Like everyone else, Turner kept going' (p. 242).

A war back home

Back at home, the nurses in England suffer routine discomfort from chilblains, hard work and emotional and physical exhaustion. McEwan depicts the horror of the battlefield most clearly through the injured hospital patients. During Robbie's journey through France, there has not been space to contemplate the detail of the wounds sustained by others, except those of a few injured civilians, but here they are laid bare in all their horror. No part of society is untouched, and no characters in the novel remain unaffected by the war. Even Emily, closed off in her private world of pain and privilege, bemoans the loss of railings and the evacuees disrupting life at the Tallis house.

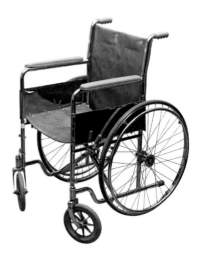

Study focus: 'The unavailable future' **A02**

The agony for Briony and her colleagues is in seeing and dealing with these injuries. The nurses do good for the soldiers, but at untold cost to themselves. Their innocence, optimism and youth are lost to the war. Briony is traumatised by her encounter with the fatally wounded Luc Cornet, whom, in another future, 'the unavailable future' (p. 311), she could have fallen in love with. This is one of the possible future worlds that are presented throughout *Atonement*.

Revision task 8: The language of war **A02**

Make brief notes on the specialist words and terms that McEwan uses in Part Two to provide realism in his depiction of the war. Make sure you check the meaning of any unfamiliar terms.

A war preserved

In 'London, 1999', the war is embodied in the Imperial War Museum. McEwan depicts Briony depositing the letters in the museum, **symbolically** fixing the war in history, with the portentously named 'Keeper of Documents' (p. 353). Yet in a novel in which the relationship between the past and the present is so closely examined, this locking away of a momentous past event is far from closing it off. The novel presents us with a sample of the myriad experiences that made up the political and military event of the war and demonstrates how the repercussions of these extend to the present time of the narrative's close; the war is certainly not over and done with in any final sense.

Briony is wrong when she says that once all the people in her tale are dead their history will no longer be real. The letters of Nettle, Robbie and Cecilia are preserved in the museum and will bear witness to the past. Briony incorporates the old colonel's corrections to military detail, describing his 'pointillist approach to verisimilitude' (p. 359); McEwan is suggesting that there are different ways of constructing the 'truth' – for the Keeper of Documents, the truth is embodied in minute factual detail about berets and artillery. A pointillist artist creates a picture through a sequence of tiny dots. However, for Briony this is not really what is important about remembering a war. Its real history is in the lives and memories of those who have experienced it and the lasting effect it has on communities.

Key quotation: War (A01)

The depiction of war in Parts Two and Three of the novel fleshes out the abstract numbers of Jack Tallis's ministry report (p. 149), realised in a sequence of horrific injuries and experiences that make us painfully aware of war's magnification of the same agony thousands of times over. Paul's plan to profit from the war – 'There'll be one of these inside the kitbag of every soldier in the land' (p. 61) – looks particularly repellent when we see the suffering that has formed the foundation of his wealth.

A03 KEY CONTEXT

Just as the First World War disrupted the strict social hierarchy that preceded it, so the Second World War removed the last vestiges of that social structure. The new, postwar social order depicted by McEwan is exemplified in the West Indian taxi driver who confounds Briony's outmoded expectations and shows, perhaps, something worthwhile salvaged from the carnage. As Robbie says, 'the ploughing would still go on and there'd be a crop, someone to reap it and mill it, others to eat it, and not everyone would be dead' (p. 235).

Love

Misspent love

Briony's family is largely dysfunctional. Emily says she loves her children, but it is an ineffectual love, never visibly resulting in any benefit or care. Emily says, of her love for Briony, 'To love her [is] to be soothed' (p. 65), which reveals Emily's selfish attitude towards her love for her children. Briony and Cecilia love each other, but their love is squandered and destroyed by inappropriate actions. Cecilia adores and admires Leon at the start, but realises that he is a 'grinning, spineless idiot' (p. 209). The only love left is the core love of Cecilia and Robbie, which nothing can alter: they 'knew their future was together' (p. 207). It is Robbie's love for Cecilia that keeps him alive in prison and in France. There is, for him, only love or oblivion.

An honest portrayal of love

It can be difficult to portray love, and especially tenderness, in a novel, without it becoming sentimental. McEwan avoids this pitfall. The change in Robbie and Cecilia's relationship from friends to lovers begins in awkwardness and antagonism. Their episode of passion is so intense it is aggressive, and the description of the sex astonishingly eloquent and sensual; Robbie is so transported that he sees himself on a 'mountain summit' (p. 138). But there is embarrassment and fumbling – he had 'trapped her where the shelves met at right angles' (p. 123) – and the interruption by Briony adds **bathos**. The lovers' heightened sensual awareness during dinner keeps the emotional charge and tension alive, extending it for hours.

KEY INTERPRETATION (A05)

McEwan has said that in writing *Atonement* he wanted to see if it was still possible, in the late twentieth century, to write a novel about love. *Atonement* is about many other things too, but love remains a central theme.

Study focus: A tribute to love (A01)

A reader might wonder how much chance Cecilia and Robbie's love would really have, limited as it was to a single episode of interrupted love-making and then an extended correspondence from prison. McEwan addresses this in the tea Robbie and Cecilia share in London before he goes to war, where they both understand the 'artificial' (p. 205) nature of the passion in their letters. But in the end it barely matters whether they could have lived happily ever after. Their story has become a fiction, but also an atonement and a tribute. As Briony says, they would soon all be forgotten anyway, without the book, and then what difference would it make 'what *really* happened' (p. 371)? Instead she makes their love transcend death by writing them a happy ending in which 'the lovers survive and flourish' (p. 371). Through this, the novel – hers and McEwan's – stands as a testament to love, and in that it deserves the ending which best suits its enduring purpose.

Key quotation: Love (A01)

By the time Cecilia and Robbie are seen together again in Part Three, their love has the weight of worldly experience behind it and has been hard-won through years of waiting and suffering. They have earned the right to compare themselves with the 'tragic couples' (p. 204) of history, recited in their letters, such as 'Tristan and Isolde, the Duke Orsino and Olivia' (p. 204) and so on. The two are united by this great love of literature.

Writing and imagination

Becoming a writer

The process of writing is itself a central concern of *Atonement*. The novel is an extended study of its own composition, and includes its own history from a burgeoning idea, a 'daily romance' (p. 38), through critical input from the editor of *Horizon*, discarded drafts, the marshalling of evidence and the process of fact-checking 'the relevant pages of my typescript' (p. 359) to its final completion. The novel is also about the making of a writer. Briony's earliest attempts at fiction are the moralistic tales she writes as a small child.

A complex, technical process

Writing involves more than imagining other consciousnesses. It must be a combination of story, characters and suitable style. Briony goes overboard in deciding to ditch story completely and follow the path of the **stream of consciousness** and impressionistic writings of the early twentieth-century **modernists**. In Cyril Connolly's phrase, she is in danger of 'throw[ing] the baby of fictional technique out with the folk-tale water' (p. 313). Although we do not get to see all of the story Briony has sent to *Horizon*, remnants remain, corrected, in the final version of the novel. This final version does indeed satisfy 'a childlike desire to be told a story, to be held in suspense, to know what happens' (p. 314), as well as show us what it is like to be someone else.

The role of a writer

As a young girl, Briony is only a writer in training. Language does not yet come naturally to her, so that she sometimes chooses inappropriate words and images. She wants order, a moral message and a pleasing logic in a **narrative** and does not consider unruly reality to be suitable subject matter. Divorce, she believes, is a 'mundane unravelling' (p. 8) that 'belong[s] in the realm of disorder' and is not 'a proper subject' (p. 8). Nor is she aware yet that the writer and reader must work together in the act of creation. The writer provides the starting material, but must release it for readers to build on. Briony complains that in performance her play has been 'defaced with the scribble of other minds' (p. 36), not realising that the involvement and cooperation of players and audience is the point of drama. All these points, though made through the portrayal of Briony's character, are points about writing as an activity and the role of the writer – of all writers, from the young Briony to McEwan himself.

Study focus: Making sense of other people

Immediately before she sees the scene at the fountain, Briony has been wondering about consciousness, and the link between mind and body, intention and action. It is an important passage for the analysis of writing as well as of Briony's development. Briony wonders, 'Was being Cecilia just as vivid an affair as being Briony?' (p. 36). She reveals that 'she knew it was overwhelmingly probable that everyone else had thoughts like hers' (p. 36), even though it makes her think the world unbearably crowded if two billion consciousnesses are operating as actively as her own.

A successful novelist

For Briony to succeed as a novelist, she has to be able to imagine herself fully inside the consciousness of another. She finally achieves this in presenting *Atonement* from the points of view of several of the characters – several centres of consciousness. We are convinced, reading Robbie's account of northern France, for example, that we can see it as he saw it. This infuses even trivial incidents, creating the psychologically real landscape of the novel. When Cecilia instructs Danny Hardman to take up Paul's suitcases, for instance, the older Briony has her wonder if he was 'interested in Lola' (p. 48). This makes it credible, later, that Cecilia thinks Danny probably attacked Lola.

A03

KEY CONTEXT

McEwan has said that writing fiction is 'about showing the possibility of what it is like to be someone else. It is the basis of all sympathy, empathy and compassion. Other people are as alive as you are. Cruelty is a failure of imagination' (interview with Kate Kellaway, 'At Home with His Worries', *The Observer*, 16 September 2001; also available at www. theguardian.com). For Briony, her increasing powers of empathy bring about her grief and regret at her false accusation of Robbie and its devastating consequences.

A02

Progress booster: A shifting narrative structure

It is important to be able to see how McEwan has structured the **narrative**, so at times we see events through future eyes. The younger Briony, watching Robbie and Cecilia at the fountain, says that Robbie 'imperiously' raised his hand (p. 38). This is how it *appeared* to the young Briony, but the older Briony knows it was *not* an 'imperious' gesture. McEwan gives the older Briony the ability to imagine herself into her younger skin – he is imagining himself into a **narrator** imagining another narrator imagining a third character's mind. It is like a nested set of Russian dolls, and a supreme achievement.

The moral value of literature

Atonement has a very real purpose for Briony. The question of the use or purpose of literature generally is raised at several points in the novel. In despair, Robbie thinks there is no point to it: 'what did the poets know about survival?' (p. 264). Yet literature sustains him, and when he imagines his future life it is filled with books, with the literature that makes him civilised and human. McEwan believes firmly in the moral value of literature and has said that being able to imagine oneself as someone else is the key to compassion.

A01

Key quotation: Writing and imagination

It is when Briony witnesses Cecilia and Robbie at the fountain that the possibility of more sophisticated writing opens up for her. It is a moment of imaginative awakening, and a rite of passage. She feels that she is being initiated into an alien world that is impossible to understand, and certainly impossible to sum up in the simple, moralistic tales she has been writing. Note how McEwan describes this moment:

> Briony had her first, weak intimation that for her now it could no longer be fairy-tale castles and princesses, but the strangeness of the here and now, of what passed between people, the ordinary people that she knew. (p. 39)

Truth and memory

Fact and fiction

In the **epilogue** at the end of the novel, Briony says that there will always be readers who ask 'But what *really* happened?' (p. 371). In a sense, it is a meaningless question because they are questioning a fictional text. The novelist, however, answers that 'what really happened' is that the lovers live happily together – not because that is what happened in historical reality, but because that is what she has written, and so it is what happened in her novel.

What is 'true'?

In the working out of the action of the novel, what is true is a central problem. It is not true that Robbie raped Lola, but it is, to a degree, true that Briony believed he did. It is not true that she saw him, but a lot hinges on her understanding of the word 'saw'. The police officer tries to clarify this, insisting on asking what she saw with her own two eyes. Briony is not to be let off on a **semantic** technicality – she lies about this. There are different types of untruth in the novel, with varying moral consequences; Lola and Paul are blatantly untruthful. Briony lies about what she saw but is truthful about what she believed. Jack Tallis does not openly tell Emily about his affair, but both characters know the 'truth' of their marriage.

Study focus: Lapses and misunderstandings (A02)

Note the number of lapses of memory and failures of understanding in the novel. The French boy, Luc Cornet, believes Briony is his French girlfriend. Briony answers his question by confirming that she loves him, as no other answer is possible and at that moment she does. It is both true and untrue. Robbie, delirious in France, imagines and recalls things that are not real. Emily wrongly thinks that Paul Marshall is good with children. Cecilia and Robbie are convinced that Danny Hardman was really the rapist. What is the effect of all these cross-communications on the 'truth' of the novel?

A declining mind

Briony reveals at the end of *Atonement* that she has vascular dementia and is losing her memory and other mental faculties. How reliable has she been as a storyteller? How much did she really remember? In the epilogue, Briony also reviews the advice she has had about details of military history. She reflects that this type of minutiae is not what a novel is about: 'If I really cared so much about facts, I should have written a different kind of book' (p. 360). Briony's point that it is not the business of a novel to present detailed historical fact suggests a way of approaching *Atonement*. The 'truth' it tells is a truth about, and distilled from, human experience and therefore immeasurably more valuable and important than tiny technical details.

Key quotation: Truth and memory (A01)

In a novel that claims to be constructed from events remembered from the past, memory is closely entwined with truth. Has Briony remembered accurately? If she has made up details, is she lying? The question of whether fiction is a lie has a long philosophical history. Sometimes, she steps in as narrator and acknowledges that she does not remember: 'it was not the long-ago morning she was recalling so much as her subsequent accounts of it' (p. 41).

A03 KEY CONTEXT

Briony writes her novel as a way of exploring the truth of her life and experiences. McEwan himself also says, 'I wanted to play with the notion of story-telling as a form of self-justification, of how much courage is involved in telling the truth to oneself' (Ian McEwan, interview with Jonathan Noakes, in Margaret Reynolds and Jonathan Noakes, *Ian McEwan: The Child in Time, Enduring Love, Atonement* (Vintage, 2002), p. 20).

Events and their afterlife

A novel about consequences

In many of McEwan's novels and short stories a brief event has vast, unimaginable consequences and completely changes the course of characters' lives. Because *Atonement* is Briony's attempt to account for and redeem herself, the unpicking of events is a central theme. The novel explores how such an event comes about as well as its consequences.

Cause and event

It is not just we as readers who question characters' interpretation of events. Robbie wonders if Briony's childish crush on him lies behind her accusation; Cecilia thinks she and Robbie are awkward with each other because of their different social class. Different characters sometimes suggest different causes and even versions of the same event. There are many instances of characters (especially Cecilia) wondering about a moment, how it will look from the future, and what its impact will be. There are false futures anticipated, which spin off small **narratives** of their own. These prefigure the largest 'what could have been' of all, Part Three.

Study focus: McEwan's narrative disruption

A02

One effect of the tendency to look forward in time is to disrupt the **narrative tension** that depends on our desire to know what happens. Sometimes McEwan gives a hint of the future with sufficiently little detail to whet our appetite and increase tension. This happens at the beginning of Chapter Thirteen: 'Within the half hour Briony would commit her crime' (p. 156). Elsewhere in Part One, it deflects our curiosity from what happens on to how and why it happens.

Events almost without meaning

In Parts Two and Three, the narrowed focus shows just what happened, with no attempt to tease out the significant events or explore how they might have a future life – the future is no longer important as the novel revolves around the false accusation. The war is too enormous for the task of analysis to have any hope of success, and is the ultimate lesson in the senselessness of what happens. As Briony has said (p. 40), events have no meaning. Lola's marriage to Paul is inexplicable, and Briony makes no attempt to unpick it. It is another story.

Knowing the future and the past

The **epilogue** casts doubt on all that the novel appears to have said about events and their reverberations through history. The detailed plan of Part One accounts only for its own key point, the moment when Briony says 'I saw him' (p. 181). It does not secure a single path for the future. The future of Part Three is as plausible as that of the epilogue. The reversal – Cecilia and Robbie dying – undermines the **determinism** that Part One apparently promotes. The future cannot be known, but no more can the past.

KEY CONNECTION   A04

At the beginning of *Enduring Love*, the **narrator** says 'I'm lingering in the prior moment because it was a time when other outcomes were still possible' (Jonathan Cape, 1997, p. 2). The opening chapters of *Atonement* are extended in the same spirit.

KEY QUOTATION   A01

As the dinner guests set out to search for the twins we lurch into the future to see how Robbie will reflect on his choice to search alone; 'This decision, as he was to acknowledge many times, transformed his life' (p. 144). Here McEwan uses the narratorial voice to telescope time in order to suggest how one thing might lead to another. Notice how the future intrudes again as Briony talks to Lola on the island and we see how she will reiterate her claim that she saw Robbie again and again until it is unchangeable.

PROGRESS CHECK

Section One: Check your understanding

These tasks will help you to evaluate your knowledge and skills level in this particular area.

1. What are the differences and similarities between Cecilia and Briony as two sisters?
2. What role does Leon Tallis play in the novel?
3. List four examples of misunderstandings and false beliefs.
4. Identify four ways in which embarrassment or humiliation is significant in the novel.
5. What is the thematic significance of the twins Pierrot and Jackson Quincey?
6. Write a paragraph explaining the significance of classic literature in *Atonement*.
7. What do Robbie Turner's experiences in France in Part Two reveal about him? Identify four aspects of Turner's character.
8. Write a paragraph exploring the significance of love as a theme in *Atonement*.
9. What role do the Tallises' servants Danny Hardman and Grace Turner play in the novel? Make two points for each character.
10. Identify three statements that show Briony's opinions about writing.

Section Two: Working towards the exam

Below are three tasks which require longer, more developed answers. In each case, read the question carefully, select the key areas you need to address, and plan an essay of six to seven points. Write a first draft, giving yourself an hour to do so. Make sure you include supporting evidence for each point, including quotations.

1. Briony chooses to write the novel from viewpoints other than her own at times, such as those of Emily Tallis, Cecilia and Robbie. How does this add to the narrative structure of the story and the reader's understanding of the characters?
2. To what extent is *Atonement* a love story?
3. 'Does Briony's atonement depend on Robbie's survival? Or can it be achieved through the eventual realisation of her literary ambitions – through a novel such as the one we are reading?' (Geoff Dyer, *The Guardian*, 2001). To what extent does Briony achieve atonement by the end of the novel?

Progress check (rate your understanding on a level of 1 – low, to 5 – high)	1	2	3	4	5
The key actions, motives and thoughts of major and minor characters in the text					
The different ways you can interpret particular characters' words and actions					
How characterisation is linked to key themes and ideas					
The significance of key themes and ideas within the text					
How some key themes (such as the need for atonement and the role of literature in our lives) are linked to context					

GENRE

Genre through the ages

Atonement borrows from many literary genres, many of which have developed over the last two hundred years, such as the country-house novel, writing about childhood, war novels, crime-writing. Briony says that at thirteen she has 'written her way through a whole history of literature ... to arrive at an impartial psychological realism' (p. 41), and *Atonement* does something similar. The first notable country-house novels were written by Jane Austen, for instance *Sense and Sensibility* (1811). In her novels, wealthy families are described living in houses very similar to the Tallis house, with all the drama contained within. As *Atonement* unfolds, it is at times a **stream of consciousness** about growing up in the style of the **modernist** Virginia Woolf, and later a **postmodern** novel that references its own structure and **narrative** in the style of modern writers such as Julian Barnes and Salman Rushdie.

Writing about childhood

Atonement spans sixty-four years and at the start of the novel some of its characters are portrayed as children: Briony, Lola, Jackson and Pierrot. Other children who feature include the victims of war in France in Part Two and the grandchildren who perform Briony's play in 'London, 1999', but none of these is a major character.

There are many classic novels that feature children and could be usefully compared to *Atonement*. *The Go-Between* by L. P. Hartley (1953) features a young boy called Leo who could be compared to Robbie Turner. As a boy from a poor background, Leo becomes the welcome member of an upper-class family of a school friend. Leo could also be compared to Briony Tallis, as he becomes the unwitting messenger between two lovers, just as Briony does for Robbie and Cecilia.

Study focus: The child in an adult world **A04**

The idea of the child as a link between adults can also be found in *What Maisie Knew* (1897) by Henry James. Maisie is a young child who is forced to move between divorced and bitterly opposed parents. Like Lola Quincey and her siblings, Maisie is forced to confront adult weaknesses at an all-too-young age. It can be argued that Maisie, like Lola, has been inappropriately sexualised as she is exposed to and involved with the affairs and marital breakdowns of the adults around her. *What Maisie Knew* can be seen as Henry James's criticism of a kind of decadence and morally weak behaviour that he observed in English society at that time – the kind of behaviour shown by Emily and Jack Tallis, who have largely abdicated their parental responsibilities, as well as Lola's parents.

Atonement as war novel

Novels that explore the effects, experiences and aftermath of wars are part of a wide literary genre. Joseph Heller's *Catch-22* (1961) is arguably the most famous Second World War novel, and presents a disillusioned catalogue of horror centring on a single character's determination to survive, in a manner analogous to Robbie Turner's ignominious wartime experience.

Atonement as crime-writing

Crime-writing – in novels, plays and poetry – is a genre that deals with the committing, detection and impact of crime and criminal behaviour. It is often traced back to the short stories of Edgar Allen Poe, such as *The Murders in the Rue Morgue* (1841), which features a detective and a terrible series of unsolved murders. However, crime-writing is a complex genre that takes many forms: from the detective story to the psychological thriller, the noir novel, legal fiction and so on. There is always a crime at the heart of these texts, however, and at the heart of *Atonement* are a rape and a false accusation leading to a prison sentence: classic features of crime-writing.

Progress booster: The narrative structure of crime-writing

Make sure you can write about how McEwan borrows from and echoes other texts within the genre of crime-writing. Shakespeare's *Hamlet* (1599) is a text that features a character whose life is consumed by the knowledge of a crime committed, although he is not the criminal; the young prince Hamlet knows that his father was murdered by his uncle, but he is unable to easily find revenge or justice. The structure of the play revolves around Hamlet's desperate guilt and indecision over how to resolve this tragic situation.

Crime-writing and social class

The Murder of Roger Ackroyd (1926) is a classic crime novel by Agatha Christie and portrays the impact of crime within upper-class society. The novel features both a murder and blackmail, with suspicion falling on working-class characters such as the butler and a young man, Ralph Paton, who has joined the family of the murder victim through marriage rather than through a natural tie – just like Robbie Turner, his position in the social hierarchy is problematic, which renders him suspicious. Robert Browning's poems 'My Last Duchess' and 'Porphyria's Lover' (1842) also examine crime in a high-class setting where privilege and power can shield the real perpetrators and allow terrible crimes, even murder, to go unpunished, as happens to Paul Marshall. By contrast, the poem 'Peter Grimes' (1810) by George Crabbe portrays the effect of crime on an isolated fishing community.

Crime and innocence

Brighton Rock (1938) by Graham Greene deals with working-class organised gang crime, but its link to *Atonement* can be seen most clearly in the close psychological examination of its main protagonists, Pinkie Brown, Ida Arnold and Rose the waitress. The effects of crime on not just the direct victims but also the innocent can be seen through the narratives of Rose and Ida as they become more and more involved with the psychopathic Pinkie, just as the innocent Robbie, Lola and Cecilia are all affected by Paul and Briony's behaviour in *Atonement*.

A05 KEY INTERPRETATION

Part Three of *Atonement* is about Briony growing up and trying to resolve her difficulties with Robbie and Cecilia. There is action, but its importance lies in what it shows us about the process taking place within Briony. It owes a lot to the tradition of rites of passage or coming-of-age novels. There are many writers who have dealt with this type of subject – it is the mainstay of the English novel, and can again be seen in novels such as Jane Austen's *Northanger Abbey*, for example.

A05 KEY INTERPRETATION

The Bildungsroman is a novel that tells the story of an individual's journey from childhood to adulthood, like *Jane Eyre* (1847). *Atonement* certainly tells the story of Briony's journey to adulthood, but has so many gaps in her life and changes of narrator that it does not neatly fit into that category.

STRUCTURE

How is *Atonement* organised?

Atonement is divided into three discrete parts and an **epilogue**, a structure that reflects movements in time and space and concentration on different characters. There is some symmetry to the pattern: we begin with all the characters together at the Tallis house, with attention focused on Briony. In Parts Two and Three, the **narrative** divides so that we concentrate on Robbie in France and Briony in London, with Cecilia as a background presence in both. Finally, the stories come together again to end back in the family house, with Briony at the centre and the remaining surviving characters around her.

The three parts of *Atonement*

The division of the main text into three parts allows McEwan to concentrate on key moments in time and place without the need to fill gaps or account for passing time. The novel could have been written very differently, showing how Briony came to feel guilty, how Robbie changed, what his life was like in prison, what Cecilia has done in the meantime. Instead, we see what happened and then are shown moments of what looks like **resolution**, for example, when Briony describes herself saying 'I'm very sorry' (p. 348) to Robbie and Cecilia at the end of Part Three and agreeing to carry out their wishes to overturn Robbie's conviction. Many of these supposed resolutions turn out to be probably fictitious or unclear in reality, as Briony admits in 'London, 1999'.

Progress booster: Different narrative structures

Be aware that Part One is quite different from Parts Two and Three in several ways. It is divided into numbered chapters, whereas the other parts offer continuous narratives with only slight pauses to indicate a change of scene or passing time. It is related from different points of view, whereas Part Two is told almost entirely from Robbie's point of view and Part Three and 'London, 1999' almost entirely from Briony's point of view. It is important that you can explain and evaluate the different effects that this has on the reader's understanding of events and characters.

Indistinct viewpoints

The multiple voices throughout Part One give this part its elusive, hazy quality. It is difficult to pin anything down – everyone sees differently, and for the greater part nothing much is happening anyway. We see everything as though through a heat haze – shimmering, with indistinct edges, just like Emily Tallis looking through 'the worn fabric of the visible world' (p. 63).

The actual incidents are not seen head-on at all, but glimpsed or recalled later. We do not see the attack on Lola, only the aftermath in the dark, which Briony at first wonders if it is 'some trick of darkness and perspective' (p. 164). This wording is interesting in that many events in *Atonement* could be linked to a **metaphorical** inability to see clearly by the characters involved. The fact that Briony, who relates it, does not see it is the key point. The other important episode, the love-making in the library, we also see at its end, again in dim light, and then in Robbie's flashback.

Study focus: Tiny incidents

Tiny incidents take on great importance in Part One, arguably because there is little else to concentrate on in this privileged and isolated community. The play, begun and abandoned, and the broken and repaired vase are the trivial details of everyday life. They are important momentarily to the people involved, although hardly the material from which great novels are built. But even these small events have their significance.

A single voice

The change to a single voice in Parts Two and Three and 'London, 1999' gives these parts a more clearly defined focus. There is more action, and it is right before the reader's eyes – brutally so, in many places. We see events taking place as Robbie sees them in France, not obscured by darkness or filtered through interpretations. The leg in the tree comes as a shock; the 'blackness' (p. 259) of the cellar appears empty to the reader as well as to Robbie until he describes 'a point of light' (p. 259) made by a cigarette.

The reader is carried along by the impetus of the action; the only movement through time now is in Robbie's reflections and hopes. What happens is presented sequentially, at a steady pace that matches the relentless onward motion of his trudge to Dunkirk, although other characters suggest scraps of other stories going on around that could be told but are not. There is no time for other people's stories, and little space for compassion: 'Like everyone else, Turner kept going' (p. 242).

Progress booster: A widening field of view

Notice how the novel expands its area of action as it progresses. From the claustrophobic setting of the Tallis house and garden, it moves in Part Two to a journey through the French countryside. Part Three is set in an extended area of London, with Briony taking us on a journey around many different parts of the city. 'London, 1999' takes the reader back to the Tallis home, now significantly altered. Think about the way the changes in landscape reflect the changes in the characters' lives and relationships.

The messiness of real life

'London, 1999' includes an admission that some of the novel is 'untrue'. This changes the structure so that technically the end of Robbie and Cecilia's story is really between parts of the novel and between England and France. The messy, frustrating lack of resolution is the very thing Briony tried to avoid in her childhood stories. Once again, she has used fiction to impose an order and rightness to events that they do not really have.

A03 KEY CONNECTION

In Henry James's novel *The Golden Bowl* (1904) a flawed crystal bowl is similarly used as a symbol, and is smashed before the end of the novel, in a manner similar to Uncle Clem's vase. Other **symbolic** objects in literature include Piggy's glasses in William Golding's *Lord of the Flies* (1954) and the dropped handkerchief in Shakespeare's *Othello* (1603).

A04 KEY CONNECTION

A good example of a traditional epilogue, used to tie the ends of a work together, achieving resolution and coherence, is the 'Note' at the end of *Dracula* by Bram Stoker, which replaces the trauma of the preceding chapters with a picture of perfect marital bliss. Stoker goes so far as to say, 'Every trace of all that had been was blotted out' (Wordsworth Classics, 2000, p. 315). McEwan deliberately subverts this form, and with it our own ideas about the novel itself.

LANGUAGE

Briony's self-consciously literary style

The young Briony's point of view is expressed in language that reflects her literary aspirations and her keenness to add new words to her vocabulary. Her cousins are from the 'distant north' (p. 3), a phrase that recalls the language of children's stories; and divorce is the 'dastardly antithesis' (p. 9) of order, two words that she has clearly taken from a dictionary or **thesaurus** rather than come across in context. Briony enjoys words but McEwan occasionally provides a humorous note when she uses such 'flowery' language, for example, marriage is 'nuptials' (p. 7) and the cousins' vivid hair colour is 'virtually fluorescent!' (p. 10).

In relating events, Briony casts them into a story with literary self-consciousness, imbuing actions with weighty significance: 'Robbie imperiously raised his hand now, as though issuing a command' (p. 38). Many writers would argue that an effective writer allows his or her readers to interpret the action; however, the young Briony wants to keep full control of how her story is received. This reduces the role of readers and consequently their interest and engagement. Briony says later that she knows how to describe but not how to convey, and this is borne out in her style.

The importance of objects

Cecilia's style is packed with detail. It works hard to recreate a picture of events and environment. She did not just hurry across the park, but 'half ran' (p. 18) through a landscape itemised in detail. She uses arresting images created by unexpected choices of words: she has a 'blossoming need for a cigarette' (p. 18) and her ancestors are 'irretrievably sunk in a bog of farm labouring' (p. 21). Some of the images are apposite and evocative, some less so. It could be argued that McEwan is conveying the style of a writer who is deliberately working, and it can feel slow to read, as even small details cannot be glossed over.

Study focus: Proper nouns and specialist language A01

McEwan often pays attention to factual detail, underpinning the realism of the novel. Notice the use of proper nouns and the correct architectural, cultural, horticultural (and so on) terms – 'Bernini's *Triton*' (p. 18), the 'faded Chesterfields', the 'almost new Gothic fireplace' (p. 20), the 'genius of Horoldt' (p. 29) and so on. It may be helpful to consider whether this language is simply a reflection of the Tallises' privilege and education, or whether it is a way of distancing the reader from this very inaccessible and specialist world.

Revision task 9: Linguistic devices A01

Notice the literary and linguistic devices that McEwan uses, and their effects. For example, **personification** and **anthropomorphism**, such as Cecilia's flowers that 'refused to fall into the artful disorder she preferred' (p. 45). The choice of the verb 'refused' has the effect of suggesting that the flowers are deliberately defying Cecilia, which causes her frustration. **Metaphors** such as the 'honeyed light' (p. 46) also play a role in conveying the unusually bright warmth and sun. Make notes on McEwan's use of imagery in *Atonement*, finding four or five examples of your own.

KEY CONNECTION A04

The style in which Briony describes Cecilia in Part One is influenced by the writing style of Virginia Woolf, a point picked up in Cyril Connolly's critique of Briony's early draft. In particular, the style of *The Waves* (1931) and *To the Lighthouse* (1927) seems to inform Cecilia's intense and **lyrical** style. Woolf's essay 'Modern Fiction' (1919) set out her idea that the point of fiction was to present the internal life, a plan which allowed any amount of introspection, which reminds the reader of *Atonement*.

Robbie's style in Part One

It could be argued that McEwan portrays Robbie as more reflective in style than Cecilia. Instead of trying to recreate every detail of every scene, Robbie develops the important aspects in greater depth. Against Cecilia's literal and metaphorical dash through the landscape, which introduces her style, Robbie spends a paragraph recreating, vividly, the exact quality of the light and the changing sky as the sun sets (p. 78). He, too, speaks of a geometric shape of window letting in the light:

> Above him the framed rectangle of sky slowly shifted through its limited segment of the spectrum, yellow to orange, as he sifted unfamiliar feelings and returned to certain memories again and again. (pp. 78–9)

Unlike Cecilia, he does not choose especially decorous or ostentatiously poetic language. He uses the language of everyday life and of science, with rectangles, spectra and segments.

McEwan may be suggesting that Robbie has more depth, that he can capture the world in language in a way that Cecilia cannot. Further evidence for this could be that Robbie earned a first-class degree in English and Cecilia only a third.

Narrating the war

McEwan conveys the details of the war in northern France through attention to sensual and immediate detail, for example the way Robbie's 'mouth and nose and ears were filled with dirt' (p. 237) after the Stuka attack. The **juxtaposition** of details from normal life alongside the alien and horrific makes the war real – the terrible shreds of pyjama fabric near the leg in the tree, the farmer sheltering from the air raid as though from rain. The style is pared down, with no explanation of psychological action.

Key quotation: Synesthesia

Sometimes, a striking image is effective for reasons that are hard to capture. Robbie finds that his 'sugared almond tasted of [Briony's] name which seemed so quaintly improbable that he wondered if he had remembered it correctly' (p. 262). This could be a strange type of **synesthesia** created by his fever, so that taste sensations are experienced as sounds. However, this kind of imagery appears elsewhere in the book, such as the 'liquid birdsong' (p. 35) heard by Briony, and is a common metaphorical device.

Progress booster: Narrative tension

Look at the way McEwan builds tension through his use of **narrative**. When Robbie goes to retrieve Nettle's boot, the language takes us through the approach to, and recognition of, the corpse. At first we, like Robbie, do not know what we are going to see: 'a black furry shape that seemed, as he approached, to be moving or pulsing' (p. 245). We share the gradual recognition with Robbie. First it looks 'furry', then as he approaches it seems to move or, more precisely, pulse. Then the bluebottles become visible and the rotting corpse is revealed (p. 245). Using only the most ordinary words, McEwan has recreated Robbie's experience of spotting something indistinguishable, puzzling over it and seeing it resolve into a recognisable form, its gross reality uncovered with a stark shock. The impact of the experience is recreated in us, not described in Robbie.

Briony's literary style

Briony's early style is analysed in detail in Cyril Connolly's letter. Although he is describing an earlier draft, traces of it remain in the finished Part One. The striking image of the 'leonine yellow of high summer', which Connolly commends (p. 312), survives in the current version (p. 38), linking the two versions like an umbilical cord. Connolly's criticism of the overly ornate, impressionistic prose must have caused Briony to cut down her description, as the episode now occupies only a few pages rather than over a hundred.

Study focus: The omniscient narrator **AO2**

The idea of the '**omniscient narrator**' is that there is a single voice or narrator who knows everything that happens and relates it accurately. Charles Dickens, for example, writes as an omniscient narrator, with access to all of his characters' thoughts. Many writers, such as McEwan, challenge that idea and use narrators that often make mistakes and do not know everything that happens. Briony can be seen as both a flawed bystander and an omniscient narrator; she positions herself as all-knowing and sometimes uses a fluent and neutral voice, carrying no obtrusive character and no emotional load, though she sometimes pauses to pass comment:

> Even without their attention and praise and obvious pleasure, Briony could not have been held back from her writing. In any case, she was discovering, as had many writers before her, that not all recognition is helpful. (p. 7)

This is assured but dispassionate prose, robbed of any emotional engagement by the passive voice ('could not have been held back'), the generalisation that places her with 'many writers before her', and the slightly dismissive 'In any case'. Make sure you can write about the different voices McEwan employs in the novel and in particular the complex narrative voice of Briony.

KEY CONTEXT **AO3**

The French philosopher Henri Bergson (1859–1941) distinguished two levels of consciousness, one reached by deep introspection which is the seat of creativity and free will, the other an outward expression of this. He won the Nobel Prize for Literature in 1927. This link between psychology and creative writing is raised by Cyril Connolly in his examination of Briony's writing – where complex 'Bergsonian theories' are contrasted with the 'childlike desire to be told a story' (p. 314).

Briony's final voice

In 'London, 1999', Briony steps out of her literary context and drops the voice of novelist/narrator to use a conversational rather than literary style:

> This, as they used to say, was the side on which her bread was buttered. That may sound sour, but it went through my mind as I glanced across at her. (p. 358)

It is a fluent, articulate and mature style. The easy use of the colloquial **idiom**, 'the side on which her bread was buttered', the direct address and anticipation of the reader's reaction create a sense of familiarity and intimacy that display a relaxed, confident relationship with language. There are far fewer literary devices or instances of 'flowery' language than there are in Part One. It could be argued that Briony's need to control her readers' response is no longer important. She can now justify and explain herself without ambiguity. The novel has found its final voice.

PROGRESS CHECK

Section One: Check your understanding

These tasks will help you to evaluate your knowledge and skills level in this particular area.

1. 'At its heart, *Atonement* is a crime novel.' Give two reasons for and two reasons against this idea.

2. To what extent is *Atonement* a novel about children and childhood? Make three or four clear points in your answer.

3. Give four reasons why McEwan divides the book into the sections he has chosen.

4. Chapter Six and Chapter Twelve in Part One are written from Emily Tallis's point of view. How does this allow the reader to see the family from different perspectives? Make three points with evidence.

5. Find three examples of Briony's deliberately literary language in Part One and briefly explain your choices.

6. In Part One, Briony says of her false accusation of Robbie, 'she marched into the labyrinth of her own construction' (p. 170). What is McEwan conveying about Briony's situation through the **metaphor** of the labyrinth? Write a short paragraph in answer.

7. What is the significance of the word 'maniac' in Part One? Write a paragraph in answer.

8. Find two or three examples of Leon's idiomatic language and 'brotherly banter' (p. 129). How does Leon's language reflect his personality?

9. How does the language of Briony's play *The Trials of Arabella* (p. 16, pp. 367–8) reflect her immaturity as a writer? Give two words/phrases as examples and provide a comment on each quotation.

10. Uncle Clem's vase has significance in *Atonement* as it relates to family history. What significance do the following objects have: the flowers that Cecilia picks; the nettles that Briony slashes; the temple in the garden?

Section Two: Working towards the exam

Below are three tasks which require longer, more developed answers. In each case, read the question carefully, select the key areas you need to address, and plan an essay of six to seven points. Write a first draft, giving yourself an hour to do so. Make sure you include supporting evidence for each point, including quotations.

1. In what ways does 'London, 1999' change our understanding of the novel we have read so far?

2. Of Part Two, McEwan has said, 'I'm not going to write about the Dunkirk evacuation. I'm going to write about Robbie trying to get to the beach' (*The New Yorker*, 2009). Explore the ways in which McEwan creates **narrative tension** in Part Two of *Atonement*.

3. In 'London,1999', Briony explains that she invented the hospital that she describes herself working in, claiming that is 'the least of my offences against veracity' (p. 356). How important is realism and factual detail in *Atonement*?

Progress check (rate your understanding on a level of 1 – low, to 5 – high)	1	2	3	4	5
How McEwan structures the novel					
How language contributes to characterisation					
How an individual text can modify our understanding of a genre					
The narrative effect of the change in point of view					
The use of specialist vocabulary and references to obtain an effect of realism					

CONTEXTS

Historical context

Study focus: Preparing for war

Part One is set in the run-up to the Second World War. Jack Tallis is portrayed as working for a ministry in London, planning for 'the mass evacuation of large towns, the conscription of labour' (p. 149) as well as calculating potential for 'five million casualties' (p. 149). Paul Marshall anticipates great profits to be made from selling 'the Army Amo' (p. 62) bars as provisions for soldiers. As Prime Minister Winston Churchill remarked in a speech in 1939, 'a terrible process is astir': Nazism was on the rise. Even so, many people hardly believed another world war could break out so soon, and we see the contrasting attitudes to the coming war played out amongst the characters in Part One. Make sure you can draw on your contextual knowledge when writing about this section of the novel – although it is less obviously dominated by war than Parts Two and Three, it nevertheless sits in the shadow of the First World War and is influenced by the new conflict that looms on the horizon.

Second World War, 1939–45

The Second World War broke out in September 1939 when the German forces, under the direction of Adolf Hitler, invaded Poland. Britain and France had an agreement to defend Poland and declared war on Germany on 3 September 1939. Other European powers quickly became involved but the German army was better organised and better equipped than the Allied (French, British and Polish) forces, leading to a protracted and devastating war right across Europe and the world.

The Dunkirk evacuation

Robbie Turner is caught up in the famous evacuation of troops from northern France in the face of immense German military power. The evacuation began on 26 May 1940; the British navy pressed small craft into service, some of which were little more than rowing boats and life rafts. Despite the terrible risks involved, these boats were used to ferry soldiers from the beach at Dunkirk to the troop carriers waiting further out at sea. A total of 198,000 British and 140,000 French and Belgian soldiers were rescued by the evacuation through Dunkirk and more through other ports to the west.

Social context

How is 'class' defined?

Class is based on socioeconomic distinctions. In the middle of the twentieth century, there were three broad classes in English society: the upper class, the middle class and the working class. The upper class traditionally comprised the nobility and landed gentry; the Tallises are not quite at that level. The upper middle classes, to which the Tallises belong, generally acquired their money through some form of business – for the Tallis family, it is patents and lock-making. They enjoy many of the lifestyle privileges of the upper class but less social prestige. Jack Tallis, as a senior civil servant, works at a high level within the government but has no personal power. Cecilia and Robbie are privately educated and sent to Cambridge University; Emily Tallis has a leisurely and pampered life. If he had lived to become a doctor, Robbie too would have been a member of the middle class.

English social class

English society had a rigid class system for many centuries. Although the divisions had no legal foundation, it was difficult for people to move between classes. The class structure at the time of *Atonement*'s action was more rigid than it is now, although the terms 'upper class', 'middle class' and 'working class' are still in use to some degree today.

The working class

At the other end of the spectrum, working-class people owned and earned little and worked in menial and often unskilled jobs. Robbie and Grace Turner are members of the working class, though Robbie's education has given him some social mobility. Betty the cook and the Hardmans are also important members of the Tallis household, but hold an uneasy relationship with the Tallises; for example, Betty openly argues with Emily Tallis over abandoning her roast meal in favour of a salad (p. 105) and Danny Hardman is suspected of assaulting Lola largely because of his lower-class origins, it seems. By the end of the novel the house has been converted into a hotel and the Tallis lifestyle has all but disappeared.

A03

Study focus: Old and new money

Consider the tension that McEwan describes when people from different classes and economic backgrounds meet. Traditionally, 'old money' – wealth handed down through the family – was considered more prestigious than 'new money' – wealth made recently through trade and industry. Paul Marshall, with his ambitions to make a great deal of money out of manufacturing confectionery, would be considered vulgar. Robbie laughingly calls Paul Marshall 'The chocolate millionaire' (p. 26) and Marshall is portrayed as being awkward and predatory. In giving Hardman a tip of five pounds, he is being ostentatious, another sign of vulgarity in English society.

A03 KEY CONTEXT

Emily Tallis suggests that Jack's support for Robbie Turner comes from some 'levelling principle' (p. 151). The idea of 'levelling' social classes is about creating more equality in society and was an important force behind the English Civil War (1642–51), for example. Emily Tallis, as a typical member of the upper middle classes, is deeply suspicious of such an idea.

Robbie Turner's social status

The importance of class in *Atonement* rests on Robbie's status as a working-class person, and the tension that his social mobility has created. While Jack Tallis has recognised Robbie's ability and paid for his education, Emily Tallis believes that it was unnecessary and inappropriate to help in this way, wondering if Robbie is merely a 'hobby' (p. 151) of Jack's and 'unfair on Leon and the girls' (p. 151). For Emily, movement between social classes is not to be encouraged and Robbie's 'elevation' (p. 152) is troubling to her.

Social status in the army

In the army, too, Robbie's status is ambiguous. He is not an officer, but Nettle and Mace defer to him because he has useful skills (map-reading, speaking French) and has the education and social veneer of an upper-middle-class man. The men have a practical attitude towards military status and do not follow orders when they consider them unreasonable (p. 220).

A new social structure

The changes in the class structure of Britain since the time when the novel is set are made clear in 'London, 1999'. A pertinent example of this is when Briony makes assumptions about Michael, 'a cheerful West Indian' (p. 362) taxi driver who is actually a law graduate.

Revision task 10: Social class and education **A02**

In an article for *The Observer* ('The Story of His Life', 23 January 2005), Robert McCrum quotes McEwan as saying ' "children who receive the education their parents did not" ... are set "on a path of cultural dislocation". ' Make notes on the ways in which Robbie, Briony and Cecilia all go on to live very different lives from their parents.

Settings

The Tallis family house

The Tallis house is **symbolic** of the family's success. Significantly, the Tallis money has been made in 'patents on padlocks, bolts, latches and hasps' (p. 19), which may suggest to the reader the locked-down and exclusive nature of their lives. During the war, the house is forced to take in evacuees, causing irreversible upheaval (p. 278). The house's conversion to a leisure facility and hotel is symbolic of the changing social structure in England.

Northern France, 1940

In the spring of 1940, German troops swept quickly across northern France and turned towards Calais and Dunkirk to cut off the ports through which British troops could be evacuated. British troops then converged on Dunkirk in a chaotic panic; it is in this historical event that Robbie Turner fights to survive. McEwan details the devastating effect the war has had on a country that was only just recovering from the First World War. This pastoral setting has become a scene of carnage in which 'one field of cattle had a dozen shell craters' (p. 214).

London

McEwan presents the capital city in two very different contexts; in 1940 and in 1999. Briony witnesses the effect of the war on London and senses the 'muted dread' (p. 284) in the city. Modern-day London in 1999 is the centre of publishing, wealth and academia; it is where Briony has lived her life as a writer, and the Marshalls their life of power and industry. However, Briony returns once more to the Tallis house (now renamed 'Tilney's Hotel') to find some final **resolution** with her childhood.

Literary context

Intertextuality

Atonement is heavily influenced by the traditions of nineteenth- and twentieth-century literature. This means there are references and **allusions** to other works which occur throughout *Atonement* (**intertextuality**) and depend for their effectiveness on us, as readers, having some familiarity with the history of English literature. *Atonement* makes sense without this knowledge, but recognising the references gives the experience of reading the novel a richer texture.

A connection to Charles Dickens

Hard Times (1854) by Charles Dickens has interesting connections to *Atonement*. The three sections of *Hard Times* are called 'Sowing', 'Reaping' and 'Garnering', which links to a quotation from the Bible (Galatians 6:7), 'For whatsoever a man soweth, that shall he also reap.' This conveys Dickens's interest in the development and growth of children into adults, which is a major theme of both *Hard Times* and *Atonement*.

In *Hard Times*, Dickens satirises the educational idea espoused by superintendent Mr Gradgrind that 'Facts alone are wanted in life!' The children in this novel, Louisa and Thomas Gradgrind, are emotionally and spiritually deprived and are symbolic of the worst of Victorian attitudes to children. As the reader follows their journey to adulthood, the reader sees the impact of their childhood, just as the reader sees the impact of Briony's and, to a lesser extent, Lola's childhood experiences at different points in their lives.

The influence of James Joyce

The action of Part One is set in a single day, a device used by many writers and extolled by Aristotle as 'unity of time'. The most famous 'single-day' novel of the twentieth century is *Ulysses* by James Joyce (1882–1941). This presents every detail, humdrum and more important events, in the lives of three characters in Dublin. Like *Atonement*, it contains complex literary allusions and includes much trivia as well as some explicit sexual content.

A postmodern conclusion

A typical feature of **postmodernist** writing is that it may look at itself and draw attention to the text's own construction, examining its structure, purpose and process. Writers such as Umberto Eco and Franz Kafka have been influential in pushing the boundaries of **narrative** in this way and it has been the concern too of **poststructuralist** critics such as Roland Barthes and Jacques Derrida, who argue that texts are constructed by the reader rather than the writer. *Atonement* can be seen as a postmodern novel in the way it first presents a novel and, in the final chapter, re-presents the novel as a book written by Briony Tallis – a character within the novel itself. Another postmodern feature is having two alternative endings – which Briony does with the possible deaths of Cecilia and Robbie during the war.

A03 KEY CONTEXT

Intertextuality is a term coined by academic Julia Kristeva (1980), which points to the way one text can refer to many other texts through quoting, **parody**, allusion and so on, suggesting that books are never fully written in isolation from one another. McEwan makes explicit and implicit references to many other writers and stories throughout *Atonement*, making it a very intertextual book.

A04 KEY CONNECTION

Cecilia's reference to *Clarissa* (1847) by Samuel Richardson is not coincidental – *Clarissa* is notable because it is an epistolary novel, or a novel written entirely in letters. In *Atonement*, several important points of plot and character are presented through letters, and there is one important letter in each part of the novel. Letters and notes are also important in *The Murder of Roger Ackroyd* (1926) by Agatha Christie and in *What Maisie Knew* (1897) by Henry James.

CRITICAL INTERPRETATIONS

Critical reception

Reviews and reaction

Atonement (2001) is a relatively recent novel, and criticism and essays about the novel still continue to be written and published. It was reviewed extensively when it was published and received a few more notices when it was nominated for or awarded various prizes. In addition, McEwan (see portrait, right) has given several interviews and written articles himself on the subject of his life and work. These are the most useful for background information on the novel and on McEwan's intentions in writing it.

Reviews on the publication or nomination of a novel generally aim to give a flavour of the book and set it in the context of the writer's other works, and they are often a good place to go to in order to learn about different readers' insights into the book. An excellent appraisal of the reviews and some more scholarly articles on *Atonement* is Peter Childs, *The Fiction of Ian McEwan: A Reader's Guide to Essential Criticism* (Palgrave Macmillan, 2006). Online journals and newspapers also offer archived reviews, essays and interviews, such as *The Guardian* and *The Paris Review*. Ian McEwan's own website has a list of reviews and study texts, some of which have online links.

What the critics say

Hermione Lee, professor of English literature at the University of Oxford, draws attention to the way *Atonement* explores a larger political topic in showing how twentieth-century society was shattered and remoulded by the Second World War and the events surrounding and following it ('If Your Memories Serve You Well', *The Observer*, 23 September 2001). Academic Frank Kermode explores the similarity with Henry James's *What Maisie Knew* (1897), a novel about family turmoil and break-up and the impact this has on a young girl ('Point of View', *London Review of Books*, 4 October 2001, pp. 8–9). Geoff Dyer compares *Atonement* to the novels of D. H. Lawrence and looks at its upper-middle-class setting ('Who's Afraid of Influence?', *The Guardian*, 22 September 2001).

Earl Ingersoll ('Intertextuality in L. P. Hartley's *The Go-Between* and Ian McEwan's *Atonement*', *Forum for Modern Language Studies*, July 2004, pp. 241–58) has looked in depth at *Atonement*'s relationship with *The Go-Between* and other texts. He examines not just the possible influences on McEwan but also the effect *Atonement* has had on our reading of other novels, including those written before *Atonement*. Making the point that the existence of *Atonement* alters a subsequent reading of *The Go-Between*, or even *Lady Chatterley's Lover*, Ingersoll draws attention to what a reader brings to a book and how our own prior experience and knowledge shapes what we find in it. This approach, following the lead of **postmodern** schools of criticism (see below, p. 95), ascribes at least equivalent importance to the reader's response as to the author's intention.

KEY INTERPRETATION **A05**

Ian McEwan: The Essential Guide, by Margaret Reynolds and Jonathan Noakes (Vintage, 2002), offers a series of reading and thinking activities to help exploration of the text.

KEY CONNECTION **A04**

The Work of Ian McEwan: A Psychodynamic Approach by C. Byrnes (Pauper's Press, 2002) looks at how McEwan's life has been reflected in his work.

Contemporary approaches

Ian McEwan and critical theory

Atonement presents an interesting case for critics because McEwan is aware of the developments in literary theory and criticism during the twentieth century and works some of them into his novel. The writer of the novel is self-consciously working within a tradition of **modernism**, **structuralism**, **poststructuralism** and postmodernism, and it could be argued that the book plays with and questions such critical approaches.

Atonement and modernism

Modernist fiction, which is generally regarded as beginning around the 1900s with writers such as Joseph Conrad and Virginia Woolf (whom Briony cites as an influence), is often described as 'experimental'. It may not have a linear or 'realistic' plot (which had been a mainstay of nineteenth-century fiction) and instead presents a more fragmented **narrative** approach. These unusual structures and ways of telling stories (starting at the end, having multiple **narrators**, shifting in time and so on) reflect what modernists saw as the way the individual is alienated by society's structures, restrictions and expectations.

Part One of *Atonement* follows a conventional narrative pattern, though takes a modernist approach in its style, particularly in the way the same event (such as Robbie and Briony by the fountain) may be reported differently by two different characters. Part Two develops the modernist style further, with the only narrative action being Robbie's journey. This is used as a canvas for reflection and a container for his **stream of consciousness** narrative, becoming increasingly experimental as his delirium disrupts any logic, such as Robbie's fevered wish to 'Gather up from the mud the pieces of burned, striped cloth' (p. 262) and bury the boy whose severed leg he sees in the tree.

Part Three explores Briony's mental state as she trains as a nurse, and so has a clearer chronological narrative structure than Part Two, although Luc's delirious fantasising arguably recalls that of Robbie in Part Two. The disjointed series of horrors seen through Briony's exhaustion during the sequences in the hospital form an almost dream-like experience floating outside the realm of normal life. 'London, 1999' changes into a first-person 'factual' narrative, with much less of a sense of the dream worlds that are explored earlier in the novel.

Atonement and postmodernism

Postmodernism is a literary movement that took the ideas of fragmentation and narrative disruption even further; postmodernist writer William Burroughs used a 'cut and paste' technique in which he tore up his writing and reordered it randomly, for example. Various meanings may then emerge from the different organisation of these fragments, and from looking at elements in different **juxtapositions**; this puts the construction of the text's meaning in the hands of the reader rather than the writer. Postmodernist writers call attention to the artificial nature of their constructions, and often mix real historical figures and events with their fictional characters, to disorientating effect.

It is possible to see reflected in Briony's development as a writer, and in the progress and structure of *Atonement* itself, the shift from conventional narrative to modernism and from there to postmodernism. McEwan could be mimicking the development of literary theory in microcosm in the approaches that he and Briony try out.

A05 **KEY INTERPRETATION**

'There are surely no accidental word choices. McEwan's writing is lush, detailed, vibrantly colored and intense' (David Wiegand, 'Stumbling into fate', *San Francisco Chronicle*, 10 March 2002). Some critics have suggested that McEwan is 'wordy'; others suggest that the detail in *Atonement* is an essential part of the narrative style. It is helpful to be able to see both sides of such arguments.

KEY CONNECTION **A04**

In *S/Z*, translated by
Richard Miller (Blackwell,
1990), Roland Barthes
famously offers an intricate
dissection of a short story
called 'Sarrasine' by the
French writer Balzac. In
S/Z, Barthes demonstrates
how language works on
many levels in the
construction of a fiction.
Although it is immensely
detailed, the text is freely
available online and is
worth looking at, to get an
idea of the level of
structuralist analysis it is
possible to go into when
trying to understand a text.

Progress booster: Mixing the real and the constructed **A02**

Cyril Connolly's letter to Briony about her short story introduces a **postmodern** awareness of the novel's own process of composition and this part of the book ends with Briony resolving to write the novel we have just read. McEwan also gives the book a postmodern aspect by having a fictional character interacting with a real historical figure. 'London, 1999' is thoroughly postmodern in its deconstruction of the whole of the preceding text and even itself, and a critical reader should be able to see how this section unpicks the novel and forces us to think about the task of composition and the roles of writer and **narrator**.

Atonement and the deconstructionist approach

Deconstructionism is a twentieth-century French philosophy that reminds us that any text we read is mediated through the language it is written in. This is problematic because language is always changing its meaning as society and individuals change. We cannot assume that what we take to be the 'truth' can always be so. Deconstructionism therefore entails very close reading of texts, thinking carefully about the context of their production. This is referred to when Briony discusses the 'truth' or otherwise of her construction, *Atonement* itself:

> I can no longer think what purpose would be served if, say, I tried to persuade my reader ... that Robbie Turner died of septicaemia at Bray Dunes on 1 June 1940, or that Cecilia was killed in September of the same year. (p. 370)

Briony's difficulty forces the reader to reflect on this choice – the happy ending has provided a hundred pages of enjoyable and stimulating, coherent fiction whereas the 'truth' dismisses the lives of Cecilia and Robbie in a single dissatisfying sentence. We are likely to choose, with Briony, the fiction. In doing so, we become complicit in the deception, the preference for 'untrue', aesthetic story over dreary truth. The art of the novelist triumphs over the book's deconstruction.

Reader-response theory: A 'writerly' or a 'readerly' text?

Roland Barthes (1915–80) describes texts as being either 'readerly' or 'writerly' (or both). A writerly text involves readers in creating its meaning, to make choices and decisions and interpret rather than being restricted by a single meaning imposed by the author. *Atonement* could be seen to fall into this category when Briony describes the history of its writing and Cyril Connolly comments on how it might be written before the final version is started. Briony herself begins as a writer of readerly texts with 'all fates resolved and the whole matter sealed off at both ends' (p. 6) and prefers not to have her creations 'defaced with the scribble of other minds' (p. 36). But she ends by undermining authorial responsibility and giving us the choice of which ending to prefer, or whether to hold both in uneasy tension.

The role of the reader

Who we are and what we believe and understand about the world will affect the way we read any text. Wolfgang Iser (b. 1926) suggests that any reader's response is equal to that of any other, whether or not it takes account of the social context of composition, the author's intentions (in so far as they can be discovered) or the work's position in, or relation to, the literary **canon**. A postmodern critic does not require meanings to have been placed in the text by the author; instead, a postmodern critic believes that meaning is discovered by the reader. This means that ultimately it does not matter whether McEwan himself shares any of the ideas raised through this type of reading, and that any reading of *Atonement* is constructed by the individual reader.

Marxist readings

Karl Marx (1818–83; see portrait, right) was a political academic who examined the economic structures of society and the causes of inequality. **Marxist critics** relate literary works to the social conditions that produced them and are reflected within them. A Marxist critic would find much to say about the social inequalities in the England of the 1930s and 1940s that led to Robbie's imprisonment. The fact that the capitalist, money-driven Paul Marshall escapes suspicion could be linked to his wealth, while the working-class Robbie Turner is convicted and then sent to war. Shifts in social and economic structures brought about by the upheaval of the Second World War lead to changes in the finances of the Tallis family – who are very much part of the bourgeoisie – such as the development of the Tilney Hotel. Briony and Cecilia remove themselves from the bourgeois circumstances of the Tallis house by become 'workers' as nurses.

Ian McEwan has always been politically engaged and often comments on world events. The social and political conditions of the 1990s when McEwan wrote *Atonement* included the aggressive dominance of the US in world politics, the social inequalities in European and American society and the way prejudices relating to race, ethnicity or religion helped to blind people to the humanity of others. In the 1990s there were conditions of anxiety and insecurity in the postcolonial UK and neocolonial US; events such as the First Gulf War (1990–1) led to great global unrest. It could be argued that conditions felt similar to the time of the Weimar Republic (the uneasy German state that existed between the two world wars) and interwar Europe. A Marxist critic may ascribe to *Atonement* an intention to comment on the sociopolitical situation of the 1990s by refracting it through the lens of the 1930s and 1940s.

A feminist reading of *Atonement*

Feminist critics look at the representation of women in literature and the way this reflects social attitudes to women. With Briony as the central character, traced from childhood to old age, there is plenty of material for a feminist reading. In Part One of the novel, Briony is disempowered by the male and adult authority figures who do not deal appropriately with her. Feminist readings may also look at the disempowered Emily Tallis: she is subservient to her absent and unfaithful husband who is able to behave as he does with impunity. McEwan explores the developments in professional status, education and independence for women in the twentieth century through Briony and Cecilia. More traditional attitudes towards women are displayed by the soldiers Nettle and Mace through the use of gendered language such as 'crumpet' (p. 193) and the division between male doctors and female nurses in the London hospital in Part Three.

Study focus: Briony as creator

It could be argued that Briony seizes power for herself by reconstructing history according to her own perception and purposes when she composes *Atonement*. This gives her an absolute role as creator, although she is troubled by the moral implications of this: 'How can a novelist achieve atonement when, with her absolute power of deciding outcomes, she is also God?' (p. 371). McEwan makes an interesting point by implying a woman can be 'God', a traditionally male construction.

A05 KEY INTERPRETATION

'[McEwan's] initial, discarded notion about *Atonement* was as a futuristic novel in which the upper class was backward looking, as if living in the 18th century, and the working class reaped the benefits of technology. The hero, Robbie Turner, would have implants in his brain and mental access to the Internet' (Mel Gussow, 'A Cool Writer Warms Up', *New York Times*, 23 April 2002). This fascinating idea gives the reader a glimpse into McEwan's main concerns in *Atonement* – the English social-class structure and the effects of moving between classes.

A02

Study focus: Metalanguage

Metalanguage is the language a book might use to talk about itself, and examples of this can be found in *Atonement* as a literary novel. McEwan's concern with the text itself as an arrangement of words and structures is paramount. He explores both the large-scale concept of fiction and story and the detail of individual words. *Atonement* includes not only a **metanarrative** in the frame which the **epilogue** gives to the whole tale, but a metalanguage of its own in having both Briony and Cyril Connolly write about its construction and its style.

The signified and the signifier

Some critics, such as the early Swiss **structuralist** Ferdinand de Saussure (1857–1913), argue that there is no fixed meaning in any language. Saussure separated the 'signified' (the thought intended by a word) and the 'signifier' (the sound of the word used for it). McEwan explores the gap between words and their meanings, which undermines the possibility not just of a meaningful metalanguage but of fixed meaning in any language. This gap is used by McEwan in making the meaning(s) of the word 'saw' central to *Atonement*: 'So when she said, over and again, I saw him, she meant it ... What she meant was rather more complex than what everyone else so eagerly understood' (p. 169).

How the novel is put together and how it works, from the level of the metafiction to the ambiguous meaning of a single word, cannot be summed up simply, or analysed using just one of these critical approaches.

New Historicist criticism

New Historicism is an analytical movement that was developed in the 1980s and 1990s by the academic Stephen Greenblatt. It involves a way of analysing works of art and literature by examining their wider cultural context and looking at them alongside many different kinds of non-fiction and non-literary texts.

A New Historicist would take as a starting point that *Atonement* was written in the late 1990s but much of it is set in the 1930s and 1940s. They would then look at some of the assumptions and knowledge a writer from the 1990s would bring to a depiction of England in 1935 and northern France in 1940. Dunkirk, for example, as depicted in Part Two, is an ambiguous event in European history. Although it is often celebrated for the bravery of the people who helped the soldiers escape France, New Historicists would be interested in the fact that McEwan, and all modern readers, would already know it was the result of the terrible power of the invading German army, and was, in fact, a chaotic defeat. A New Historicist may look at this event alongside Prime Minister Winston Churchill's 1940 speech in which he said, 'We must be very careful not to assign to this deliverance the attributes of a victory. Wars are not won by evacuations.'

PROGRESS CHECK

Section One: Check your understanding

These tasks will help you to evaluate your knowledge and skills level in this particular area.

1. List three actual historical events/people in the novel and comment briefly on their significance in the **narrative**.

2. Identify three working-class characters and briefly note their significance in the novel.

3. Find three aspects of the Tallis house and gardens that symbolise their social status.

4. 'The social structure of England has changed enormously by "London, 1999".' Find two pieces of evidence to support this statement and two to argue against the statement.

5. Write a short paragraph about the significance of the London hospital setting for the development of Briony as a character.

6. Make a list comparing three characteristics of Cecilia's lifestyle in Part One and the very different world in which she finds herself in Part Three.

7. Write a short paragraph outlining the ways in which Briony is influenced by **modernism** and particularly the works of Virginia Woolf.

8. Identify three aspects of the text that could be seen as **postmodern**.

9. List four aspects of the book that are concerned with money and could provide material for a **Marxist** reading.

10. List three ways in which a **feminist** reading of the character Emily Tallis could help us understand women's lives in the upper middle classes in the 1930s.

Section Two: Working towards the exam

Below are three tasks which require longer, more developed answers. In each case, read the question carefully, select the key areas you need to address, and plan an essay of six to seven points. Write a first draft, giving yourself an hour to do so. Make sure you include supporting evidence for each point, including quotations.

1. 'Social class is less important than the "inbetween-ness" of the characters, who are often in flux and have a desperate desire to have more control of their place in the world.' To what extent would you say that social class is important in *Atonement* and in another text you have read?

2. 'Tragic heroes are created through misadventure and a fatal flaw, which causes them to fall from greatness.' How far would you agree that Robbie Turner is a tragic hero?

3. Write about the ways in which female voices are presented in *Atonement* and another text in your wider reading in the poetry of love through the ages.

Progress check (rate your understanding on a level of 1 – low, to 5 – high)	1	2	3	4	5
How some knowledge of context enhances interpretation of the novel					
The different ways the novel can be read, according to critical approaches such as feminist or historicist					
How comparison with another literary work can deepen understanding of both					
How a reader's interpretation may differ from the author's intended meaning					
How *Atonement* can be read as a historical document					

ASSESSMENT FOCUS

How will you be assessed?

Each particular exam board and exam paper will be slightly different, so make sure you check with your teacher exactly which Assessment Objectives you need to focus on. You are likely to get more marks for Assessment Objectives 1, 2 and 3 if you are studying AQA A or B, but this does not mean you should discount 4 or 5. Bear in mind that if you are doing AS Level, although the weightings are the same, there will be no coursework element.

What do the AOs actually mean?

	Assessment Objective	Meaning
AO1	Articulate informed, personal and creative responses to literary texts, using associated concepts and terminology, and coherent, accurate written expression.	You write about texts in accurate, clear and precise ways so that what you have to say is clear to the marker. You use literary terms (e.g. '**simile**') or refer to concepts (e.g. 'unreliable **narrator**') in relevant places. You do not simply repeat what you have read or been told, but express your own ideas based on in-depth knowledge of the text and related issues.
AO2	Analyse ways in which meanings are shaped in literary texts.	You are able to explain in detail how the specific techniques and methods used by McEwan to create the text (e.g. **narrative** voice, dialogue, **metaphor**) influence and affect the reader's response.
AO3	Demonstrate understanding of the significance and influence of the contexts in which literary texts are written and received.	You can explain how the text might reflect the social, historical, political or personal backgrounds of McEwan or the time when the novel was written. You also consider how *Atonement* might have been received differently over time.
AO4	Explore connections across literary texts.	You are able to explain links between *Atonement* and other texts, perhaps of a similar genre, or with similar concerns, or viewed from a similar perspective (e.g. **postmodernism**).
AO5	Explore literary texts informed by different interpretations.*	You understand how *Atonement* can be viewed in different ways, and are able to write about these debates, forming your own opinion. For example, how a critic might view Emily Tallis as **symbolic** of a declining middle class whilst another might see her as representing the repression of women's voices in pre-war England.

* AO5 is not assessed by Edexcel in relation to *Atonement*.

What does this mean for your revision?

Whether you are following an AS or A Level course, use the right-hand column above to measure how confidently you can address these objectives. Then focus your revision on those aspects you feel need most attention. Remember, throughout these Notes, the AOs are highlighted, so you can flick through and check them in that way.

Next, use the tables on page 101. These help you understand the differences between a satisfactory and an outstanding response.

Then, use the guidance from page 102 onwards to help you address the key AOs, for example how to shape and plan your writing.

Features of **mid-level** responses: the following examples relate to Briony's role in the novel:

	Features	Examples
A01	You use critical vocabulary appropriately for most of the time, and your arguments are relevant to the task, ordered sensibly, with clear expression. You show detailed knowledge of the text.	Briony is both the **narrator** and a **central protagonist**, although sections are **narrated** from the **point of view** of other characters, such as Emily Tallis and Robbie Turner.
A02	You show straightforward understanding of the writer's methods, such as how form, structure and language shape meanings.	McEwan structures the novel in **largely chronological order**, although the changing points of view have the effect of revealing detail and retelling scenes in a way that causes the reader **to question the reliability** of the narrative but also become more engaged in the exploration of the characters and their stories.
A03	You can write about a range of contextual factors and make some relevant links between these and the task or text.	The play spans the twentieth century and, through the eyes of Briony Tallis and other characters, examines the impact of the **Second World War** on the English class system.
A04	You consider straightforward connections between texts and write about them clearly and relevantly to the task.	'Atonement' is a novel that explores the ongoing impact of an unintentional crime, in the same way that '**The Rime of the Ancient Mariner**' by S. T. Coleridge explores the effects of crime and retribution and the compulsion to retell a story.
A05	You tackle the debate in the task in a clear, logical way, showing your understanding of different interpretations.	Some would argue that Briony is an unreliable narrator, **but Briony herself often reflects on the complex issue of realism** in fiction writing, even to the point of offering an alternative ending to the lives of Cecilia and Robbie.

Features of a **high-level** response: these examples relate to a task on narrative perspectives:

	Features	Examples
A01	You are perceptive, and assured in your argument in relation to the task. You make fluent, confident use of literary concepts and terminology; and express yourself confidently.	The process of writing is itself a central concern of 'Atonement' with McEwan engaging the reader in postmodern debate about the nature of fictional reconstruction of historical events, the ambiguity of characters and the changing styles of English literature, from the country-house novel to the painstakingly researched war novel aspect of 'the relevant pages of my typescript' (p. 359).
A02	You explore and analyse key aspects of McEwan's use of form, structure and language and evaluate perceptively how they shape meanings.	Robbie sees himself as 'Prometheus, chained to a rock' at his greatest moments of despair. This **conveys** the educated and sensitive nature of Robbie Turner but is also a device through which McEwan explores the **role of literature** as a signifier and filter of human experience.
A03	You show deep, detailed and relevant understanding of how contextual factors link to the text or task.	The Tallises are symbolic of the **upper middle classes in England** who occupy an uneasy divide between the **aristocracy** and the **working class**. The movement of characters between social classes creates a narrative of problematic and changing **social structures in England**.
A04	You show a detailed and perceptive understanding of issues raised through connections between texts. You have a range of excellent supportive references.	McEwan presents children becoming involved with the affairs and marital breakdowns of the adults around them; the abdication of responsibility for the Quincey siblings by their divorcing parents echoes Henry James's criticism of decadent adulthood in his novella **What Maisie Knew**.
A05	You are able to use your knowledge of critical debates and the possible perspectives on an issue to write fluently and confidently about how the text might be interpreted.	Part of 'Atonement''s structure as a **postmodernist text** is the employment of a **metanarrative**. The **postmodern structure of the novel** allows for a consideration of an alternative ending and the discussion of a draft by Cyril Connolly, although it can also be seen as **problematising the 'reliability' of Briony** as the narrator.

HOW TO WRITE HIGH-QUALITY RESPONSES

The quality of your writing – how you express your ideas – is vital for getting a higher grade, and **AO1** and **AO2** are specifically about **how** you respond.

Five key areas

The quality of your responses can be broken down into **five** key areas.

EXAMINER'S TIP

AO1 and AO2 are equally important in AS and A Level responses.

1. The structure of your answer/essay

- First, get **straight to the point in your opening paragraph**. Use a sharp, direct first sentence that deals with a key aspect and then follow up with evidence or detailed reference.
- **Put forward an argument or point of view** (you won't **always** be able to challenge or take issue with the essay question, but generally, where you can, you are more likely to write in an interesting way).
- **Signpost your ideas** with connectives and references which help the essay flow. Aim to present an overall argument or conceptual response to the task, not a series of unconnected points.
- **Don't repeat points already made**, not even in the conclusion, unless you have something new to add.

Aiming high: Effective opening paragraphs

Let's imagine you have been asked about the role of **narrators** in crime-writing. Here's an example of a successful opening paragraph:

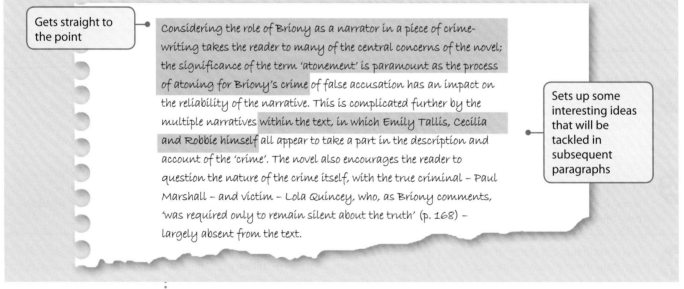

Gets straight to the point

Considering the role of Briony as a narrator in a piece of crime-writing takes the reader to many of the central concerns of the novel; the significance of the term 'atonement' is paramount as the process of atoning for Briony's crime of false accusation has an impact on the reliability of the narrative. This is complicated further by the multiple narratives within the text, in which Emily Tallis, Cecilia and Robbie himself all appear to take a part in the description and account of the 'crime'. The novel also encourages the reader to question the nature of the crime itself, with the true criminal – Paul Marshall – and victim – Lola Quincey, who, as Briony comments, 'was required only to remain silent about the truth' (p. 168) – largely absent from the text.

Sets up some interesting ideas that will be tackled in subsequent paragraphs

2. Use of titles, names, etc.

This is a simple, but important, tip to stay on the right side of the examiners.

- Make sure that you spell correctly the titles of the texts, chapters, authors and so on. Present them correctly too, with inverted commas and capitals as appropriate. For example, 'Atonement'.
- Use the **full title**, unless there is a good reason not to (e.g. it's very long).
- Use the term 'text' rather than 'book' or 'story'. If you use the word 'story', the examiner may think you mean the plot/action rather than the 'text' as a whole.

3. Effective quotations

Do not 'bolt on' quotations to the points you make. You will get some marks for including them, but examiners will not find your writing very fluent.

The best quotations are:

- Relevant and not too long (you are going to have to memorise them, so that will help you select shorter ones!)
- Integrated into your argument/sentence
- Linked to effect and implications

Aiming high: Effective use of quotations

Here is an example of an effective use of a quotation about perception in the novel:

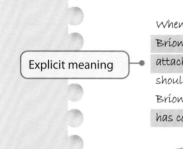

Explicit meaning

When Briony says 'The truth instructed her eyes', it is not just Briony stating that she believed that she saw Robbie Turner attacking Lola Quincey. The inversion of logical order, that the eyes should show you the truth, conveys the catastrophic nature of Briony's continued misrepresentation of Robbie as the 'maniac' who has committed such a terrible crime .

Short, relevant quotation, embedded in sentence

Inferred meaning

Remember – quotations can also be one or two single words or phrases embedded in a sentence to build a picture or explanation, or they can be longer ones that are explored and picked apart.

4. Techniques and terminology

By all means mention literary terms, techniques, conventions, critical theories or people (for example, 'paradox', 'archetype', 'feminism' or 'Plato') **but** make sure that you:

- Understand what they mean
- Are able to link them to what you're saying
- Spell them correctly

5. General writing skills

Try to write in a way that sounds professional and uses standard English. This does not mean that your writing will lack personality – just that it will be authoritative.

- Avoid colloquial or everyday expressions such as 'got', 'alright', 'ok' and so on.
- Use terms such as 'convey', 'suggest', 'imply', 'infer' to explain the writer's methods.
- Refer to 'we' when discussing the audience/reader.
- Avoid assertions and generalisations; don't just state a general point of view ('Briony's narration is unreliable because it changes throughout the book'), but analyse closely with clear evidence and textual detail.

Note the professional approach here in the choice of vocabulary and awareness of the effect on the reader:

*McEwan's use of multiple voices throughout Part One **conveys** a sense of opaque haziness. The 'vast heat' and the shifting, restless narratives seem to make it increasingly difficult to locate factual event and clear social boundaries; instead, **we** find ourselves, like Emily Tallis, looking metaphorically through 'the worn fabric of the visible world' (p. 63).*

> **EXAMINER'S TIP**
>
> Something examiners pick up is that students confuse 'narrator' and 'author'. Remember that Briony is a character as well as the narrator, and don't confuse her with the novel's author, Ian McEwan.

QUESTIONS WITH STATEMENTS, QUOTATIONS OR VIEWPOINTS

Often students are set a question on one particular aspect (e.g. Cecilia and Robbie's relationship) but end up writing almost as much about another (such as Briony and Cecilia). They are answering the question they would like to have seen! **Stick to the question set**, and answer **all parts of it**.

One type of question you may come across is one that includes a statement, quotation or viewpoint from another reader. You are likely to be asked this about *Atonement*, or about *Atonement* and another text you have studied.

These questions ask you to respond to, or argue for/against, a specific **point of view** or critical interpretation. This is likely to be in relation to the genre of crime-writing.

For *Atonement* these questions will typically be like this:

> **'Briony's crime has ultimately more impact on herself than on her perceived victims. This makes her search for forgiveness much more difficult.' To what extent do you agree with this view? Remember to include in your answer relevant detailed exploration of McEwan's authorial methods.**

The key thing to remember is that you are being asked to **respond to a particular perspective or critical view** of the text – in other words, to come up with **your own** 'take' on the idea or viewpoint in the task.

Key skills required

The table below provides help and advice on answering the question above.

Skill	Means?	How do I achieve this?
To focus on the specific aspect, by exploring McEwan's authorial methods	You must show your understanding of crime as a genre which writers use, first tackling in what ways 'forgiveness' and the significance of who the victim is are key elements of crime-writing, secondly deciding the degree to which they apply to the novel.	You will need to deal with the issue generally, either in an opening paragraph or in several paragraphs, but also make sure you keep on coming back to this issue throughout the essay, rather than diverting into other areas which you have not been asked about.
To consider different interpretations	There will be more than one way of looking at the given question. For example, critics might be divided about the extent to which McEwan suggests that Briony is forgiven.	Show you have considered these different interpretations in your answer. For example, a student might write: *Briony is able to continue a relationship with her family and to have a successful career, and through this she is able to achieve atonement. However, her rejection by Cecilia and Robbie implies her crime can never be forgiven.*
To write with a clear, personal voice	Your own 'take' on the question is made obvious to the examiner. You are not just repeating other people's ideas, but offering what **you** think.	Although you may mention different perspectives on the task, you settle on your own view. Use language that shows careful, but confident, consideration. For example: *Although it may appear that Briony has superficially suffered few repercussions from her crime, I feel that her lifetime of atonement has a similarly epic weight as that of the tragic sailor in 'The Rime of the Ancient Mariner'.*
To construct a coherent argument	The examiner or marker can follow your train of thought so that your own viewpoint is clear to him or her.	Write in clear paragraphs that deal logically with different aspects of the question. Support what you say with well-selected and relevant evidence. Use a range of connectives to help 'signpost' your argument. For example: *We might say that Briony has achieved atonement for her crime by the end of the novel. However, the fact that her book has remained unpublished has meant that no 'judgement' has been 'handed down'. Therefore, the reader is asked to question the relationship between judgement, forgiveness and atonement.*

Answering a 'viewpoint' question

Let us look at another question:

> 'Crime-writing does not always concern itself with the victims of crime.' Explore the significance of the ways in which victims are presented in two crime texts you have studied.

Stage 1: Decode the question

Underline/highlight the **key words**, and make sure you understand what the statement, quotation or viewpoint is saying. In this case:

Crime-writing: *consider the genre features and conventional aspects of crime-writing and how your texts might conform to or challenge these conventions*

Explore: *look at the different aspects, put forward a range of views and ideas*

'the significance of ...' *means what victims represent, how important they are in the text, what impact they have on the narrative and the meaning of the text*

'the ways in which victims are presented...': *this means the linguistic and literary techniques, tone, point of view, role in the narrative*

So you are being asked to identify the victims in the text, the techniques that are used to present them and how these ways of presenting the victims are important within the text.

Stage 2: Decide what your viewpoint is

Examiners have stated that they tend to reward a strong view which is clearly put. Disagreeing strongly can lead to higher marks, provided you have **genuine evidence** to support your point of view. However, don't disagree just for the sake of it.

Stage 3: Decide how to structure your answer

Pick out the key points you wish to make, and decide on the order that you will present them in. Keep this basic plan to hand while you write your response.

Stage 4: Write your response

Begin by expanding on the aspect or topic mentioned in the task title. In this way, you can set up the key ideas you will explore. For example:

Fictional victims can be presented in many ways – sometimes they can be the narrator or central character of the text as in Charles Dickens's 'Oliver Twist', or they can be in the background, with the perpetrator of the crime as the narrator, such as in 'The Rime of the Ancient Mariner'. More problematic is 'Atonement''s narrative structure, which gives a voice to both victim (Robbie) and perpetrator (Briony), when arguably the real criminal is Paul Marshall, and the real victim is Lola Quincey.

Then in the remaining paragraphs proceed to set out the different arguments or perspectives, including your own.

In the final paragraph, end with a clear statement of your viewpoint, but do not list or go over the points you have made. End succinctly and concisely.

Then, proceed to dealing with the second text in a similar way.

EXAMINER'S TIP

You should comment concisely, professionally and thoughtfully and present a range of viewpoints. Try using modal verbs such as 'would', 'could', 'might', 'may' to clarify your own interpretation. For example, *I would argue that the victimisation of the RAF man at Dunkirk symbolises the latent frustration of the British soldiers being forced to retreat. Robbie's involvement could be seen as a form of self-defence. Furthermore, it could be argued that, as narrator, and as part of her atonement, Briony chose to include this scene to honestly present the terrible moral choices Robbie is forced to make as a soldier.*

COMPARING *ATONEMENT* WITH OTHER TEXTS

As part of your assessment, you may have to compare *Atonement* with or link it to other texts you have studied. These may be other novels, plays or even poetry. You may also have to link or draw in references from texts written by critics.

Linking or comparison questions might relate to a particular theme or idea, such as 'love'. For example:

> **By exploring the writers' methods, compare ideas about the way in which passionate love can change the way we see the world, in one prose text and one poetry text you have studied.**

Or:

> **Compare the ways in which the writers of your two chosen texts present tensions in the family. You must relate your discussion to relevant contextual factors.**

You will need to:

Evaluate the issue or statement and have an **open-minded approach**. The best answers suggest meaning**s** and interpretation**s** (plural):

- For example, in relation to the first question: do you agree that love is presented in this way? Is this aspect more important in one text than in another? Why? How?
- What are the different ways in which this question or aspect can be read or viewed?
- What evidence is there in each text for this perspective? How can you present it in a thoughtful, reflective way?
- What are the points of similarity and difference?

Express **original or creative approaches** fluently:

- This isn't about coming up with entirely new ideas, but you need to show that you're actively engaged with thinking about the question, not just reeling off things you have learnt.
- **Synthesise** your ideas – pull ideas and points together to create something fresh.
- This is a linking/comparison response, so ensure that you guide your reader through your ideas logically, clearly and with professional language.

Know *what* **to compare/contrast**: the writer's methods – **form, structure** and **language** – will **always** be central to your response. Consider:

- The authorial perspective or voice (who is speaking/writing), standard versus more conventional narration (use of flashback, **foreshadowing**, disrupted time or **narrative** voice which leads to dislocation or difficulty in reading)
- Different characteristic use of language (lengths of sentences, formal/informal style, dialect, accent, balance of **dialogue** and narration; difference between prose treatment of an idea and poem)
- Variety of symbols, images, **motifs** (how they represent concerns of author/time; what they are and how and where they appear; how they link to critical perspectives; their purposes, effects and impact on the narration)
- Shared or differing approaches (to what extent do McEwan and the author(s) of Text 2/3 conform to/challenge/subvert approaches to writing about love?)

EXAMINER'S TIP

Remember that for the AQA A or B specifications in order to score highly in your answer you will also need to discuss what the critics say (AO5) and consider relevant cultural or contextual factors (AO3). AO5 is not assessed by Edexcel in relation to *Atonement*.

Writing your response

Let us use the example from page 106:

> By exploring the writers' methods, compare ideas about the way in which passionate love can change the way we see the world, in one prose text and one poetry text you have studied.

EXAMINER'S TIP

If you are following an AS course, you may have less exam time to write than for the A level – so concise, succinct points with less elaboration than provided here may be needed.

Introduction to your response

- Either discuss quickly what 'passionate love' or 'the way we see the world' means, and how well this applies to *Atonement* and two poems you have studied, or start with a particular moment from one of the texts which allows you to launch your exploration.

- For example, you could begin with a powerful quotation to launch your response:

'He touched his pocket. It was a kind of genuflection.' In Part Two of 'Atonement', Robbie Turner clings on to the memory of Cecilia Tallis's love, represented by a letter he carries in his pocket. His passionate love for Cecilia has had a transformative effect on his perception of the world. McEwan possibly uses the word 'genuflection', which literally means 'bending the knee', to convey Robbie's role as the courtly heroic lover, but also maybe to suggest a quasi-religious element to his worship of Cecilia.

Main body of your response

- **Point 1**: continue your exploration of one character's view of the world in *Atonement*: what it implies about society, how McEwan fitted it to the issues of the time in terms of the historical settings, why this is 'interesting' for readers today. How might we interpret that relationship differently through time?

- **Point 2**: now cover a new factor or aspect through comparison or contrast of this relationship with another in Text 2 and/or 3. For example, *John Wilmot, in 'A Song (Absent from Thee)', argues that it is a natural aspect of life to be separated from a loved one and a 'Fool' will 'mourn' such separation.* How is/are the new relationship(s) in Text 2 presented **differently or similarly** by the writer according to language, form, structures used; why was this done in this way?

- **Points 3, 4, 5, etc.**: address a range of other factors and aspects, for example other 'passionate' relationships **either** within *Atonement* **or** in both *Atonement* and the other texts. How do you respond to these – and why? For example:

It can be argued that there is an intense relationship between the young Briony and Robbie Turner, although it is a fleeting childhood crush. Robbie recalls a significant event when he takes Briony swimming and she pretends to drown so that she can trick him into rescuing her. This event is recounted in a dreamlike manner, with a description of 'the light that dropped like jewels through the fresh foliage', which seems to set a romantic mood, although it is clear that Robbie only has his mind on his future and he regards Briony's conversation as 'prattle'. It is a shock when Briony declares she did it 'Because I love you'. Robbie later speculates that Briony's jealous love for him leads to the 'rancour' that causes her to falsely accuse him of rape.

Conclusion

- Synthesise elements of what you have said into a succinct final paragraph which leaves the marker with the sense that you have engaged with this task and the texts.

In 'A Song (Absent from Thee)', love appears to thrive in separation, but returning is to find 'Love and Peace and Truth'; the poem presents a sense of hope that is catastrophically absent in both Blake's 'The Garden of Love' and in the 'real' story of Cecilia and Robbie, which, despite a love that 'consumed' both characters, is doomed to end as an 'unhappy inversion' as they are killed in the Second World War.

USING CRITICAL INTERPRETATIONS AND PERSPECTIVES

What is a critical interpretation?

EXAMINER'S TIP

Make sure you have thoroughly explored the different types of criticism written about *Atonement*. Bear in mind that views of texts can change over time as values and experiences themselves change, and that criticism can be written for different purposes.

The particular way a text is viewed or understood can be called an interpretation, and can be made by literary critics (specialists in studying literary texts), reviewers, or everyday readers and students. It is about taking a position on particular elements of the text, or on what others say about it. For example you could consider:

1. Notions of 'character'

What **sort/type** of person Robbie Turner – or another character – is:

- Is the character an 'archetype' (a specific type of character with common features)? (Could Robbie be seen as a romantic or war hero?)
- Does the character **personify**, symbolise or represent a specific idea or trope (Robbie Turner may represent the shifting social classes in twentieth-century England)?
- Is the character modern, universal, of his/her time, historically accurate? (For example, can we see aspects of today's soldiers in Robbie's experiences? Is Robbie more fixed in his time as the son of domestic staff who is privately funded through Cambridge University?)

2. Ideas and issues

What the novel tells us about **particular ideas or issues** and how we interpret these. For example:

- How society is structured: the English class distinctions in the first half of the twentieth century are portrayed in *Atonement*, with the legacy of the landed aristocracy traceable in the architecture of the Tallis grounds, contrasting with the income generated by the patent-developing Tallis patriarch. The broader issue of shifting social boundaries and social uncertainty can be seen in the figures of Robbie, Grace Turner and Cecilia Tallis.
- The role of men/women: in the years before the Second World War it was still socially acceptable for young women to have limited social and educational aspirations; a university education for women was sometimes seen as a waste of time and money. Figures such as Jack Tallis and Paul Marshall imply a male-dominated social order. However, the success and power that come to both Briony Tallis and Lola Quincey reflect the different choices that are available to men and women as the century develops.
- Moral codes and social justice: criminal behaviour plays a significant role in this novel, but there are also indications that such behaviour is due, in part at least, to injustice and inequality, along lines of race and gender as well as social class.

3. Links and contexts

To what extent the novel **links with, follows or pre-echoes** other texts and/or ideas. For example:

- Paul Marshall's view of children and McEwan's portrayal of the uneasy relationship between Paul and Lola Quincey could be compared with Nabokov's *Lolita* (1955) in which an older man has a relationship with a young teenage girl.
- McEwan's use of the country house and a plot partly driven by misunderstandings and complex relationships can be linked to Jane Austen's *Northanger Abbey* (1817).
- In its depiction of the experiences of soldiers in the Second World War, *Atonement* could be seen to be working in a similar genre to Joseph Heller's *Catch-22* (1961).

4. Genre and narrative structure

How the novel is **constructed** and how McEwan **makes** his **narrative**:

- Does it follow particular narrative conventions? For example, those of the **modernist** genre?
- What are the functions of specific events, characters, plot devices, locations etc. in relation to narrative or genre?
- What are the specific moments of tension, conflict, crisis and denouement – and do we agree on what they are?

5. Reader responses

How the novel **works on the reader**, and whether this changes over time and in different contexts:

- How does McEwan **position** the reader? Are we to empathise with, feel distance from, judge and/or evaluate the events and characters?

6. Critical reaction

And, finally, how do different readers view the novel? For example, different critics over time, or different readers in the early 1920s in the US, **postmodern** and more recent years.

Writing about critical perspectives

The important thing to remember is that **you** are a critic too. Your job is to evaluate what a critic or school of criticism has said about the elements above, arrive at your own conclusions, and also express your own ideas.

In essence, you need to: **consider** the views of others, **synthesise** them, then decide on **your perspective**. For example:

Explain the viewpoints

Critical view A about America's potential:

> A historicist reading of 'Atonement' might examine the way the novel sheds light upon the socioeconomic structures of England between the 1940s and the end of the century, and the way in which the 'lost memory' of the Adam-style house represents its baronial past, in contrast to the 'wooden bench' and 'litter basket' of Tilney's Hotel that signifies modern commercial power.

Critical view B about the same aspect:

> A feminist reading of 'Atonement' could look at the decline of the Tallis family as a counternarrative to the improving fortunes of women who have lived through the emancipating process of independent work and life after the Second World War. The stultifying entrapment of Emily Tallis has given way to the liberated and successful life of Briony Tallis as a writer in the public eye.

Then synthesise and add your perspective:

> Valuable insights might be gained from a historicist perspective which enables us to examine the role of minor characters such as 'Michael' the West Indian taxi driver who may signify a new form of social structure and diversity towards the end of the novel. However, McEwan has four women as central characters, and it is a feminist reading of the text that is best able to articulate the transformation in women's roles as the twentieth century undergoes huge changes. It may be argued that a feminist reading of 'Atonement' (significantly, McEwan aligns 'Atonement' very strongly with Jane Austen's 'Northanger Abbey', another novel of the female voice) carries greater weight than a historicist reading, in particular in terms of examining female transgression, sexual love and autonomy.

A05 **KEY INTERPRETATION**

Here are just two examples of different kinds of response to *Atonement*:

Critic 1 – Pilar Hildago's 'Memory and Storytelling in Ian McEwan's *Atonement*' says that 'the reader is made aware of the perils of perception' and at the same time is made aware of the 'narrative devices' in which literary texts encode experience.

Critic 2 – Hermione Lee in 'If Your Memories Serve you Well' (*The Observer*) suggests that, in McEwan's depiction of Robbie as a soldier in France, 'The bloody, chaotic shambles of the retreat sabotages one common national fantasy, of Dunkirk as a heroic rescue.'

ANNOTATED SAMPLE ANSWERS

Below are extracts from three sample answers at different levels to the same task/question. Bear in mind that these responses may not correspond exactly to the style of question you might face – for example, AO5 is not assessed by Edexcel – but they will give a broad indication of some of the key skills required.

> **Question:** 'McEwan suggests that true atonement for one's crimes can never be possible.' To what extent do you agree with this view? Remember to include in your answer relevant detailed exploration of McEwan's authorial methods.

Candidate 1

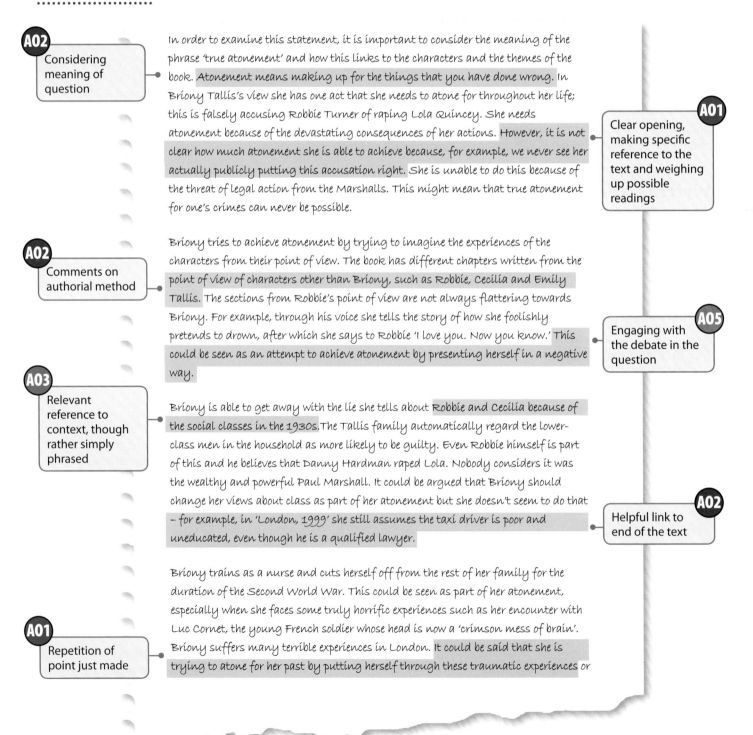

AO2 Considering meaning of question

In order to examine this statement, it is important to consider the meaning of the phrase 'true atonement' and how this links to the characters and the themes of the book. Atonement means making up for the things that you have done wrong. In Briony Tallis's view she has one act that she needs to atone for throughout her life; this is falsely accusing Robbie Turner of raping Lola Quincey. She needs atonement because of the devastating consequences of her actions. However, it is not clear how much atonement she is able to achieve because, for example, we never see her actually publicly putting this accusation right. She is unable to do this because of the threat of legal action from the Marshalls. This might mean that true atonement for one's crimes can never be possible.

AO1 Clear opening, making specific reference to the text and weighing up possible readings

AO2 Comments on authorial method

Briony tries to achieve atonement by trying to imagine the experiences of the characters from their point of view. The book has different chapters written from the point of view of characters other than Briony, such as Robbie, Cecilia and Emily Tallis. The sections from Robbie's point of view are not always flattering towards Briony. For example, through his voice she tells the story of how she foolishly pretends to drown, after which she says to Robbie 'I love you. Now you know.' This could be seen as an attempt to achieve atonement by presenting herself in a negative way.

AO5 Engaging with the debate in the question

AO3 Relevant reference to context, though rather simply phrased

Briony is able to get away with the lie she tells about Robbie and Cecilia because of the social classes in the 1930s. The Tallis family automatically regard the lower-class men in the household as more likely to be guilty. Even Robbie himself is part of this and he believes that Danny Hardman raped Lola. Nobody considers it was the wealthy and powerful Paul Marshall. It could be argued that Briony should change her views about class as part of her atonement but she doesn't seem to do that – for example, in 'London, 1999' she still assumes the taxi driver is poor and uneducated, even though he is a qualified lawyer.

AO2 Helpful link to end of the text

AO1 Repetition of point just made

Briony trains as a nurse and cuts herself off from the rest of her family for the duration of the Second World War. This could be seen as part of her atonement, especially when she faces some truly horrific experiences such as her encounter with Luc Cornet, the young French soldier whose head is now a 'crimson mess of brain'. Briony suffers many terrible experiences in London. It could be said that she is trying to atone for her past by putting herself through these traumatic experiences or

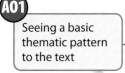

A01
Seeing a basic thematic pattern to the text

that she is trying to suffer in the same way as Cecilia and Robbie, who, as a nurse and a soldier themselves, also encounter horrific events. To this extent, I believe that Briony achieves atonement, because she has behaved in such a self-sacrificing way.

It could be argued that Briony misses an opportunity to really atone for her action when she attends Lola and Paul Marshall's wedding. By watching Lola marry the man who raped her, Briony has to reflect that if she had spoken the truth as a child then this marriage would never have happened.

A01
Rather too much retelling of the story

After the wedding, Briony goes to visit Robbie and Cecilia for the only time in the story and she tries to atone for her action face to face. The situation is very difficult for Briony because Cecilia and Robbie are so angry with her and so the communication between the three of them is very tense. When Cecilia first sees Briony she only says 'Oh my God', because she is so shocked. Robbie is very angry and Cecilia has to stop him from attacking Briony. Even though it is hard for her, Briony admits she takes 'calm pleasure' from telling them about Paul Marshall, which might mean she has achieved some kind of atonement. She then decides that she will rewrite the novel and make that her final atonement. This is a postmodern idea – to have the character write the novel that you are reading.

A01
Point is a little tenuous and unsupported

A05
Literary concept but not further developed

However, although Briony might not achieve atonement as such, she does appear to achieve some kind of happiness. She is a successful writer and she is clearly greatly loved when she returns to watch her childhood play, 'The Trials of Arabella', at the Tallis home, which is now a hotel. McEwan might be suggesting that, in time, the need for atonement fades; Paul and Lola appear to be successful and content, the Tallis family love Briony unconditionally, and Cecilia and Robbie are long dead, victims of war rather than of Briony's foolishness. So it could be argued that even if true atonement is never possible (because the memory of the crime will always be with the criminal), fulfilment and happiness are still possible.

A01
Retains focus on question

A01
Clear conclusion

MID LEVEL

Comment

- AO1 A clear and methodical approach, consistently weighing up pros and cons in a basic but consistent way. Needs to push the analysis further to move it beyond broad observations and to avoid retelling the story. Some sections could also be more clearly linked.
- AO2 Broad sense of ways in which meaning is shaped in *Atonement*. Closer attention to language and technique would have raised the level of the analysis.
- AO3 Makes reference to historical context but critical engagement with it needs further development.
- AO4 No attempt to bring in literary comparison or context.
- AO5 This answer is marked by basic yet consistent critical evaluation, which demonstrates awareness of point of view. Doesn't engage with more sophisticated critical perspectives.

To improve the answer:

- Pay closer attention to the way meaning may be shaped by use of language and literary techniques. (AO2)
- Engage more purposefully with relevant historical and literary contexts. (AO3/AO4)
- Develop a more sophisticated understanding of how critical interpretations might shed light on key issues.

Candidate 2

A02 Analysing how language shapes meaning

'Atonement' is a broad concept that will have different definitions depending on cultural and personal expectations. If we define atonement as the act of making amends for something that you have done wrong, then the reader can clearly see that Briony, the narrator and 'writer' of the book, has written the book itself as an act of atonement for her catastrophic act as a young girl. However, the word can also be read as 'at-one-ment' and the book could also be interpreted as a way to explore identity and the devastating consequences of a single act.

A01 Exploring key term

Frank Kermode said that McEwan has a 'keen interest in ... point of view' and that it is significant that McEwan chooses a young girl who is obsessed with creative writing and so produces fictions that have 'their own kind of truth'. Briony's search for atonement through the writing of the book is problematic throughout the novel to the point where it could be argued that she will never be able to achieve atonement, because she will never be fully able to articulate the truth about what happened. The subjective nature of truth is an important theme in both modernist and postmodern literature, although they deal with it in different ways, but 'Atonement' is influenced by both movements of writing.

A05 Critical response

A01 Clear argument

A02 Authorial methods linked to literary movements if rather simplistically

A01 Referring to details of text and weighing up pros and cons

Briony tries to atone by writing 'Atonement' the book, and by trying to tell the story of what she saw and believed as a young child. Her first draft, 'Two Figures by a Fountain', is rejected by the literary editor CC because there is no 'development'. CC suggests that the story would be better if the 'watching girl did not actually realise that the vase had broken' and that she needs to change her story. However, this might suggest to the reader that Briony is changing what she really saw to make her story more interesting. In which case it could be argued that she will never achieve atonement, because she may never fully reveal the truth, if in fact the truth can ever be fully known.

A02 Confident use of text

A01 Sophisticated idea, could be further developed

A05 Relevant critical interpretation

Briony makes the decision to fully rewrite the novel after the meeting with Cecilia and Robbie, following the Marshalls' wedding. As part of her atonement, Briony learns that the 'truth' is now going to be 'walled up within the mausoleum of their marriage' with the metaphor 'mausoleum' suggesting a deathlike finality reflecting what John Walsh describes as McEwan's perception of humanity's 'chilly soul'.

A02 Appropriate terminology and effect

A02 Explores ways in which meanings are shaped

McEwan also reminds us that the Marshalls were part of the conspiracy of 'silence and falsehoods' that sent Robbie to prison. It could be that Briony's atonement itself has now been sabotaged by the marriage of the 'white-faced couple' and the 'prised open' young woman. McEwan employs typically macabre language to suggest the impact the wedding has on Briony, in contrast with the rest of the family who appeared either bored or dutiful. Maybe enduring this uncomfortable spectacle is part of Briony's atonement? And maybe further atonement is made by the way Briony endures Robbie's steely anger and Cecilia's shock at her revelations straight after the wedding.

A02 Good point and apt quotations but lacking in language analysis

AO2
Focus on question

It could be argued that Briony attempts to achieve atonement by reconstructing the terrible events that Robbie endures in France. She lists the traumatic sights of body parts and 'vaporised' women and children, the petty squabbles and bureaucracy; all of these serve to present Robbie as a heroic, intelligent and courageous young man, in contrast to the violent rapist that Briony had publicly labelled him as.

AO1
Confident written style

AO5
Good personal interpretation

The conclusion to the novel is where you would usually look to make a decision as to whether Briony really achieves atonement, but there you can argue that McEwan has deployed yet another narrative trick. Briony now tells the reader that she is suffering from 'vascular dementia', which is an illness that will destroy the memory. This is ironic in a novel that has memory as a major theme, and Briony reacts in an ironic manner, saying she was 'elated', even as she reflects on the 'slowness of the undoing' of her mind. You could interpret this as a hint that Briony is already ill and so already an unreliable narrator. In fact, maybe just the fact of returning to the Tallis household and being greeted with love and kindness, rather than disapproval, is all the atonement that Briony actually requires.

AO5
Engaged argument

AO2
Analysing language feature

Briony, in the novel's conclusion, appears to decide that she cannot achieve atonement because she has 'absolute power' over the characters as if she is 'God'. Interestingly, McEwan suggests that Briony could be 'God' (with a capital 'G'), challenging the normally masculine identity of God, which may reflect Briony's status as a female novelist who has assumed the troubled role of 'omniscient narrator'. As Briony says, 'No atonement for God, or novelists, even if they are atheists.' Which raises the interesting question of the link between power and atonement; as long as you have power over your victims then you can never gain atonement; and Briony has the ultimate power of life and death over Cecilia and Robbie because 'she has set the limits and the terms' and the reader will never know 'what really happened'.

AO1
Argument informed by helpful embedded quotes but lacks a final conclusive sentence

GOOD LEVEL

Comment

- AO1 Traces Briony's development through the novel skilfully, and puts forward some different interpretations; writes clearly with focus.
- AO2 Analyses the structure of the text as a whole and shows some understanding of the effects of the complex narrative structure.
- AO3 A broad sense of the Second World War setting.
- AO4 Helpful link to modernism.
- AO5 A sense that different perspectives are invited by this text, with helpful reference to critical analysis. A clear exploration of the term 'atonement'.

To improve the answer:

- Use a wide range of literary terms and provide some deeper analysis of language. (AO1)
- Make more focused reference to historical and literary contexts. (AO3/AO4)
- Sharpen the sense of how a critical perspective shapes the interpretation of a text. (AO5)

Candidate 3

A01 Confident opening

'Atonement' is, unarguably, a literary novel and McEwan's complex construction of Briony as narrator, character, criminal and witness draws on many different genres and literary movements. However, the question asks us to reframe 'Atonement' as a crime novel, the genre conventions of which presuppose the inclusion of a criminal, a victim and a crime. Yet the shifting nature of the book's narrative and the multiple potential readings McEwan introduces invite us to question whether the seemingly simple journey from crime to atonement can be made at all. Indeed, one may ask to what extent is Briony a truthful narrator, or if, in fact, as Barthes would suggest in 'The Death of the Author' (1967), it is the reader who constructs the meaning of the text? From this point of view we must ask to what extent we can look to Briony for a true account of her crimes and her atonement or even if her story can be understood as 'true' or 'real' in any sense. Indeed, Briony herself argues that there can be 'No atonement for Gods, or novelists', suggesting that the power of creation overrides other aims. This is a book therefore that is all about perception, recording, telling and showing as much as it is about cause and effect – meaning that the very nature of the crime is problematic, as is the nature of Briony's search for atonement itself.

A02 Precise attention to the question of genre

A05 Links 'Atonement' to critical theory

A02 Integrated reference to support argument

Briony's initial attempts to explain the events of her childhood, which (we are to assume) begin her process of atonement, are submitted as a novella to CC (a fictionalisation of the real literary editor Cyril Connolly). Ironically, given her supposed search for atonement, her emulation of contemporary modernist writers such as Virginia Woolf leads her to write in a style which has 'fine rhythms and nice observations' but lacks the 'backbone of a story'. In other words Connolly's use of the idiomatic term 'backbone' suggests that the story that Briony has written does not contain a strong enough narrative thrust for it to serve as an act of atonement.

A03 Literary context

A01 Accurate terminology

It is important to note that when Briony the narrator describes her childhood self she appears to emphasise the young Briony's innocence and total immersion in unreality. In the chapter that begins 'Within the half hour Briony would commit her crime', Briony is supposed to be searching for the missing twins. She is, however, more concerned with her dreams of flying; 'this might be achieved, through desire alone', which leads her to reflect on writing 'as a kind of soaring', the choice of the word 'soaring' emphasising the height of Briony's literary ambitions. Crucially, it is only one page further on that Briony pictures Robbie as the 'brute', as she extends her flight of fancy into the 'real' drama unfolding around her. One might ask whether, rather than looking for atonement, Briony the narrator is trying to defend Briony the child by presenting her younger self's absorption in the imagined world. We might also wonder if McEwan uses this passage to ask wider philosophical questions, such as to what extent a child can commit a crime, and whether this same child can ever achieve atonement if they have no understanding of the consequences of it?

A02 Apt language analysis

A05 Different interpretations

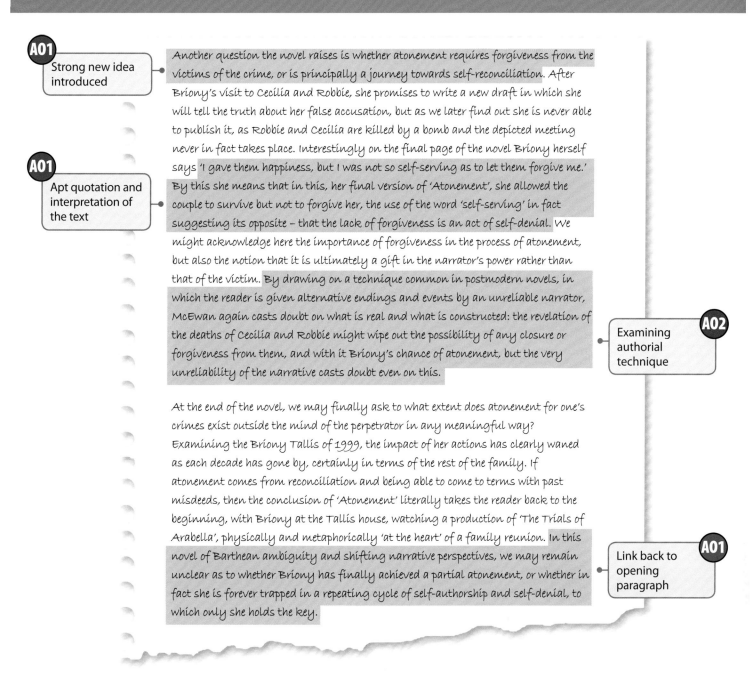

A01 Strong new idea introduced

A01 Apt quotation and interpretation of the text

A02 Examining authorial technique

A01 Link back to opening paragraph

Another question the novel raises is whether atonement requires forgiveness from the victims of the crime, or is principally a journey towards self-reconciliation. After Briony's visit to Cecilia and Robbie, she promises to write a new draft in which she will tell the truth about her false accusation, but as we later find out she is never able to publish it, as Robbie and Cecilia are killed by a bomb and the depicted meeting never in fact takes place. Interestingly on the final page of the novel Briony herself says 'I gave them happiness, but I was not so self-serving as to let them forgive me.' By this she means that in this, her final version of 'Atonement', she allowed the couple to survive but not to forgive her, the use of the word 'self-serving' in fact suggesting its opposite – that the lack of forgiveness is an act of self-denial. We might acknowledge here the importance of forgiveness in the process of atonement, but also the notion that it is ultimately a gift in the narrator's power rather than that of the victim. By drawing on a technique common in postmodern novels, in which the reader is given alternative endings and events by an unreliable narrator, McEwan again casts doubt on what is real and what is constructed: the revelation of the deaths of Cecilia and Robbie might wipe out the possibility of any closure or forgiveness from them, and with it Briony's chance of atonement, but the very unreliability of the narrative casts doubt even on this.

At the end of the novel, we may finally ask to what extent does atonement for one's crimes exist outside the mind of the perpetrator in any meaningful way? Examining the Briony Tallis of 1999, the impact of her actions has clearly waned as each decade has gone by, certainly in terms of the rest of the family. If atonement comes from reconciliation and being able to come to terms with past misdeeds, then the conclusion of 'Atonement' literally takes the reader back to the beginning, with Briony at the Tallis house, watching a production of 'The Trials of Arabella', physically and metaphorically 'at the heart' of a family reunion. In this novel of Barthean ambiguity and shifting narrative perspectives, we may remain unclear as to whether Briony has finally achieved a partial atonement, or whether in fact she is forever trapped in a repeating cycle of self-authorship and self-denial, to which only she holds the key.

VERY HIGH LEVEL

Comment

- AO1 An impressively coherent and creatively personal response. In control of materials and of the construction of a persuasive argument.
- AO2 Use of quotations has a confidence that reflects an assured grasp of ways in which meaning is shaped in the text.
- AO3 Focused and refreshing engagement with literary context.
- AO4 Secondary materials used with precision and purpose.
- AO5 Astute and assured reference to critical approaches and the light they might shed on central issues of the text.

PRACTICE TASK

Now it's your turn to work through an exam-style task on *Atonement*. The key is to:

- Quickly read and decode the task/question
- Briefly plan your points – then add a few more details, such as evidence, or make links between them
- Write your answer

Decode the question

> **'Plotting and calculation are central ingredients of crime literature.' Explore the significance of plotting and calculation as they are presented in two crime texts you have studied.**

'Plotting and calculating'	suggests considering arrangements and activities leading up to a deliberate crime – does McEwan show characters doing this?
'central ingredients'	This could invite a discussion about what makes a crime novel – are there 'ingredients' a writer must include?
'significance'	How far do I agree with this? These elements may not be significant at all in fact.
'they are presented'	This is looking at the writers' methods and techniques and the construction of the text.

Plan and write

- Decide your viewpoint
- Plan your points
- Think of key evidence and quotations
- Write your answer

Success criteria

- Show your understanding of the idea of **tragedy** as a genre
- Draw on a range of critical views or different interpretation as appropriate
- Sustain your focus on the idea of 'illusion'
- Argue your **point of view** clearly and logically
- Make perceptive points and express your ideas confidently
- Support your points with relevant, well-chosen evidence including quotations
- Use literary terminology accurately and appropriately with reference to the effect on the reader
- Write in fluent, controlled and accurate English

Once you have finished, use the **Mark scheme** on page 128 to evaluate your response.

FURTHER READING

Articles by Ian McEwan

There is a full list of articles on McEwan's website, www. ianmcewan.com

'How Could We Have Forgotten that This Was Always Going to Happen?', *The Guardian*, 8 July 2005

'Only Love and Then Oblivion', *The Guardian*, 15 September 2001

'Beyond Belief', *The Guardian*, 12 September 2001

Criticism

Margaret Reynolds and Jonathan Noakes, *Ian McEwan: The Child in Time, Enduring Love, Atonement*, Vintage, 2002

David Malcolm, *Understanding Ian McEwan*, University of South Carolina Press, 2002

Peter Childs, *The Fiction of Ian McEwan: A Reader's Guide to Essential Criticism*, Palgrave Macmillan, 2006

McEwan's website, www.ianmcewan.com, has links to reviews of and articles about his novels

Background studies

Malcolm Bradbury, *The Modern English Novel*, Secker & Warburg, 1993

Peter Childs, *Contemporary Novelists*, Palgrave Macmillan, 2005

Steven Connor, *The English Novel in History: 1950–1995*, Routledge, 1996

Dominic Head, *The Cambridge Introduction to Modern British Fiction, 1950–2000*, Cambridge University Press, 2002

Michael McKeon, ed., *Theory of the Novel: A Historical Approach*, Johns Hopkins University Press, 2000

Jago Morrison, *Contemporary Fiction*, Routledge, 2003

LITERARY TERMS

allusion an implicit reference to another work, a person or an area of experience the reader may share with the writer; allusion draws on shared knowledge

anthropomorphism assigning human features or characteristics to an animal or object

bathos moving quickly from an elevated topic or sentiment to a ridiculous, comic or banal one

canon the established body of literature

chronological account a way of telling a story so that the events are described in the order in which they take place

cliché a widely used expression which, through overuse, has lost any impact or originality

comic relief a pause in tension caused by the introduction of humour; comic relief breaks a sustained run of emotionally intense action

conceit clever or ingenious trick, such as an intricate idea or image given pleasingly imaginative expression

deconstructionist an approach to criticism which employs close analysis of a text in an attempt to unpick it and find a plurality of meanings within it. It is an application of **poststructuralism** which locates all meaning(s) within the text and does not make attempts to depend on outside influences

determinism a belief that the outcomes of action (or fate) are predetermined and cannot be altered by the operation of free will on the part of individuals

dramatic tension sustained expectation or suspense which keeps the audience or reader anxious to know the outcome of an action or situation

duality a way of including pairs and opposites in a text in order to show contrasts and links

epilogue a final section to a piece of literary writing that reflects back on the text in some way

feminist criticism criticism that seeks to describe and interpret women's experience as depicted in and mediated through literary texts

foreshadow to give an anticipatory indication, or to hint at what will follow later in the **narrative**

historical novel a novel set in a historical period, with the cultural, social, economic and/or political setting of the period playing a significant part in the development of the action and characters

identify (with a character) to emotionally align oneself with a character in a work of literature

idiom a word or phrase peculiar to a particular language and having an established meaning which often differs from its apparent or literal meaning

intertextuality explicit or implicit reference to other texts within a work of literature

irony wry humour derived from a discrepancy between words and their meaning, or actions and their outcome

jargon specialist words and vocabulary connected to a particular topic

juvenilia a writer's earlier work

juxtaposition the placing together of two or more, usually contrasting, ideas

lyrical originally meaning poetry intended to be sung, lyrical poetry expresses the emotions or thoughts of one person, often using language and rhythm that sound song-like. Lyrical prose is subjective, emotive, fluent and with features of poetic expression

Marxist criticism criticism which seeks to adapt the sociopolitical and economic ideology of Karl Marx (1818–83) to a reading methodology. After the Hungarian Georg Lukács (1885–1971), Marxist criticism concentrates on the depiction of social-class structures, struggles and injustice. Marxist criticism relates the content of a work to the social shifts it represents or which produced it. More recent Marxist critics have concentrated on the 'gaps' in a text, and on what is left unsaid, as its more revealing aspects

melodrama a form of drama in which extravagant and sensational deeds and thinly drawn characters are portrayed, with strong elements of violence, sexuality and evil and a simplistic moral or judicial code

metanarrative a **narrative** that is aware of it own status as an idea, often used as a frame for more traditional narratives

metaphor a comparison between two things in terms of their implicit characteristics; the associations can be complex and linked to culture and identity

modernism a move away from established structures and models to embrace the experimental and avant-garde in form and content

motif a minor event, image or word that is used repeatedly for deliberate effect

narrative a literary work that tells a story, or the progress of the action (story) in a literary work

narrative tension suspense created by the desire to know what is going to happen in a story or sequence of events

narrator the person or voice telling a story; an **omniscient narrator** is a narrator who has access to all the viewpoints of the characters in the story, and tells it from a third-person perspective

parody a humorous, distorted or vastly exaggerated version of a literary form (or person, character or situation) which makes the model look ridiculous. Like caricature in drawing, it is a form of mimicry with the intention of deriding the original

pastoral literature with a countryside setting

personification describing an animal or inanimate object as if it has human characteristics

popular fiction fiction that lays claim to no literary merit but which is written for a mass audience, often in a popular genre such as romance, crime, horror or science fiction

postmodernism a move into more radical and experimental forms of writing and criticism in which the forms and functions of literature are directly questioned within a work. Postmodern writing is often self-referential, and plays with the conventions and forms of established literature

poststructuralism a movement that finds fault with the premises of **structuralism** and tends to show that there are no definite and stable meanings in a text or even a word. It allows a plurality of views or meanings to coexist and denies the possibility of single, objective truth

reader-response a critical school which gives pre-eminence to the reader's contribution in constructing meaning in a text by means of what he or she brings to a reading of it

reflexive novel a novel which includes reflection on or attention to the method and process of its own composition

resolution events which form the outcome of the action in a literary work, with all problems, dilemmas and mysteries brought to completion

Romantic poet a poet writing in the tradition of Samuel Taylor Coleridge and William Wordsworth in the last years of the eighteenth and early decades of the nineteenth centuries. The English Romantic poets rejected the formal structures and ostentatiously poetic language of earlier poetry written in the classical and neoclassical traditions in order to write freely and subjectively about feelings, nature and personal experience using everyday language

Romanticism a literary movement or style that is concerned with expressing emotional responses to extreme experiences

semantic relating to the meaning of language and symbols

simile a kind of **metaphorical** writing in which one thing is said to be like another thing. Similes always compare two things and contain the words 'like' or 'as'. For example: 'the soldier was like a lion in battle'

stream of consciousness writing which presents thoughts as they occur to a character or **narrator** with no overt attempts to link or structure them

structuralism a movement concerned with the methods of communication and the ways in which meaning is constructed into signs (such as words). It finds that literature does not reflect a pre-existing and unique reality of its own but is built up from other conventions and texts

symbolic a word or image used in such a way that the reader may associate it with a particular feeling or idea

sympathetic demanding or inviting our sympathy and engagement

synesthesia describing one sense in terms of another

thesaurus a book providing alternatives to words and phrases

tragedy originally a drama dealing with elevated actions and emotions and characters of high social standing in which a terrible outcome becomes inevitable as a result of a sequence of events and the personality of the main character. Classical dramatists in Greece and Rome and later European writers such as Shakespeare adhered to this model of tragedy. More recently, tragedy has come to include courses of events happening to ordinary individuals which are inevitable because of social and cultural conditions which could and should be changed. Writers of this type of tragedy include the Norwegian Henrik Ibsen (1828–1906), and Americans Arthur Miller (1915–2005) and Eugene O'Neill (1888–1953)

REVISION TASK ANSWERS

Task 1: Misinterpretations

- Emily Tallis believes that Jackson and Pierrot will return on their own and Lola is merely attention seeking.
- Lola Quincey and the twins misinterpret Paul Marshall's interest in them as just friendliness.
- Other misunderstandings include: Robbie thinks Briony's false accusation is motivated by jealousy of his relationship with Cecilia; Briony misunderstands the 'N. Tallis' initial on her uniform.

Task 2: Depictions of pain

- Corporal Nettle throws his boots 'into a field' (p. 245) and says he hates his blisters more than all the 'Germans put together' (p. 245). McEwan identifies a very real historical point in that many soldiers suffered more from the indirect problems of lack of decent supplies and clothing than from actual threat from the German soldiers.
- The airman with shrapnel in his leg cries out an expletive as Briony is treating him; 'The escaped word ricocheted around the ward and seemed to repeat itself several times' (p. 300). The word 'ricocheted' is a suitable military **metaphor** as it is a word that means the movement of an object, such as a bullet, and shows the physicality of the soldier's pain-filled shout.

Task 3: Keeping up appearances

- Lola comes to the dinner party covered in bruises but does not reveal her distress or the fact that they were caused by Paul Marshall.
- Robbie refuses to reveal his true feelings of distress to Nettle and Mace, often choosing to hide behind the map – 'the map was his only privacy' (p. 192). This appears to be a self-defence mechanism.

- Briony does not reveal her true feelings about the marriage between Paul and Lola, even though it is a chance to set the record straight about Robbie and to 'purge herself of all that she had done wrong' (p. 325).

Task 4: Considering Lola

- Lola appears genuinely bewildered by Marshall's attacks but does not contradict Briony's accusation of Robbie, thereby condemning Robbie to prison.
- Briony accuses Lola of 'dominion' and 'obliviousness' (p. 15), which is echoed later by Emily Tallis's harsh judgement of Lola, who would 'remain guiltless while others destroyed themselves at her prompting' (p. 147).
- Briony's epithet of 'Cruella de Vil' (p. 358) is darkly humorous, although Briony admits that she is an 'unreliable witness' (p. 358) when it comes to Lola – the legal metaphor being grimly apposite.

Task 5: McEwan's portrayal of the police

- Emily Tallis expects 'deference' from PC Vockins (the word 'Vockins' actually means 'little people'), showing her adherence to class values. She finds him distasteful because he speaks in **clichés** and was a member of a trade union (p. 146) and so would have campaigned against social inequality.
- The senior inspector is portrayed using imagery that conveys his power; his face is made of 'folded granite' (p. 174) and 'ancient rock' (p. 179) – this suggests that Briony is much more in awe of him than Emily.
- The inspector makes a 'sensitively created space' (p. 180) for Briony to speak about what she has seen; this kindness and professionalism **ironically** enables her to continue with her fabrication.
- The officers are seen as 'impassive' (p. 185) when Briony watches the final exchange between Cecilia and Robbie; their reactions are in contrast to the high emotions of the family.

Task 6: Separations and divorces

- The young Briony vaguely knew 'that divorce was an affliction' (p. 8) and Jackson shocks his siblings and Briony by mentioning their parents' divorce – the word has the sound of an 'obscenity' (p. 57).
- Ernest Turner abandons his wife and child 'without even a farewell note' (p. 83), which in those days of very limited social welfare could have meant catastrophic poverty and upheaval for the young family.
- By 'London, 1999', both Leon (who is married four times in total) and Briony are widowed, whereas the Marshall's marriage has lasted for more than fifty years. Briony tells us that Jack Tallis eventually remarried and moved permanently to London.

Task 7: Brothers and sisters

- Cecilia and Leon have a close relationship; there is a detailed description of their childhood game of 'quaking torture' (p. 51) in which they try not to laugh during formal dinners. They 'squabble' (p. 53) but communicate through 'glances' (p. 54), showing their continued unity.
- Emily describes the Quincey twins as a 'four-legged creature' (p. 67) and they do seem hard to distinguish. It is commented that 'whatever happened to Jackson would be Pierrot's future too' (p. 33).
- The relationship between Cecilia and Briony as siblings is made distant by their age gap and by Cecilia's prolonged absence at Cambridge University and Briony's lack of understanding of Cecilia's inner thoughts and personality.
- Emily Tallis's relationship with her own sister Hermione (whom we never meet) is represented as problematic and critical, with Emily frequently commenting on Hermione's 'impulsive behaviour' (p. 8) in her divorce.

Task 8: The language of war

- 'Corporals' (p. 192): not the lowest rank in the army, although Nettle and Mace have no men to lead and defer to Robbie's intelligence
- 'Private soldier' (p. 193): the lowest rank in the army; Turner's actual level
- 'General conscription' (p. 195): conscription is the forcing of men to sign up to war; Robbie uses the image to describe the bees that swarm together to attack

- 'RASC' (p. 196): Nettle and Mace are part of the RASC, which organised supplies such as catering – Mace is an army cook
- 'The "bull" ' (p. 207): this was a nickname for the tough regime that saw ordinary men trained to be soldiers
- 'Panzer division' (p. 216): German tanks that were renowned for their efficiency
- 'major' (p. 220): majors could command up to 120 men

Task 9: Linguistic devices

- The windows that 'permit' sunlight to 'advance' across the room (p. 20) make a busy scene straining with energy, battling against the hot torpor of the day.
- Robbie thinks his marching shoes sound 'like a giant clock' (p. 92); although it might be a simplistic **simile**, it puts him in mind of the passing of time.
- Robbie emerging from the morning mist with the sleeping boy on his shoulders is surreally described as a giant 'seven or eight feet high' (p. 182), conveying the dreamlike unreality of the night time's events.
- The soldiers arriving at Briony's hospital are described as 'a wild race of men from a terrible world' (p. 291), conveying their dehumanised and disturbing condition, especially from the inexperienced Briony's point of view.

Task 10: Social class and education

- Robbie's dreams of being a doctor would have taken him to a higher social class than Grace his mother, and perhaps given some 'dislocation' from his background, in addition to his privileged education.
- Cecilia attends Cambridge University and would have been in the vanguard of women attending higher education; she is much more educated than Emily Tallis, and this appears to have distanced her from her mother.
- Cecilia and Briony's decision to train as nurses would have been typical of women from all social backgrounds during wartime. However, Cecilia continues to 'dislocate' herself from her social background and appears to deliberately choose a much more modest lifestyle.
- Briony may have had a different type of education from her mother, but her comments about her past in 'London, 1999' and her career as a successful and wealthy writer suggest that she has not really changed in terms of social class and could still be seen as an 'upper-middle-class' woman.

PROGRESS CHECK ANSWERS

Part Two: Studying *Atonement*

Section One: Check your understanding

1.

- For: Briony is writing the story to atone for her mistakes, so it would be unhelpful to be dishonest about events.
- For: We learn that she has taken a great deal of trouble to check facts about Robbie's experiences in the war at the Imperial War Museum (p. 353).

- Against: Briony suggests that Cecilia and Robbie died during the war.
- Against: Briony is not able to fully know what was going on in the minds of people such as Emily Tallis, so some sections of the story can only be guesswork.

2.

- Emily and Jack Tallis have a long marriage that outwardly looks successful, with well-educated and happy children and a beautiful family home.
- However, Emily has no 'wish to know' (p. 149) why Jack is away from home so often and the reader infers that he is having an affair; Jack's work at the ministry is used as an excuse by both Emily and Jack for his absence.

- Emily in response is passively unhappy and helplessly lonely at the Tallis house, whereas Jack occasionally intervenes in household events (such as the disappearance of the twins) by telephone.

3.

- Briony Tallis violently attacks the nettles with a branch (p. 74). This is her way of releasing her frustrations about her life at home and gives the reader an insight into her internal thoughts.
- Lola reports being attacked by the twins; 'They got me down on the floor' (p. 118). We later learn that she was actually hurt by Paul Marshall as a precursor to the rape that is to set off the rest of the events in the novel. This hints at Marshall's violent character.
- Mrs Turner attacks the police car as they are taking Robbie away (p. 186). Her rage is indicative of Robbie's innocence.

4.

- Divorce was very uncommon in the 1930s and the children are all understandably bewildered and upset.
- Jackson has to 'gather his courage' (p. 57) to even say the word 'divorce' and the word is regarded by the children as 'an unthinkable obscenity' (p. 57) because of the social stigma attached to it.
- The divorce has placed the children into an uncertain world in which the rules of 'The Parents' (p. 57) have become meaningless.
- With the loss of boundaries and certainties, the childrens' behaviour becomes erratic, culminating in the twins' disappearance and ultimately Lola's rape.

5.

- Paul Marshall behaves in a sinister manner when he is alone with Lola and the twins. The twins are mistrustful of him; 'they knew that an adult had no business with sweets' (p. 61).
- Paul encourages Lola to eat his chocolate bar in a suggestive manner – ' "Bite it", he said softly' (p. 62) – which is a clearly inappropriate way to speak to a child.
- Marshall speaks rudely at the dinner, talking behind Cecilia to Robbie. Robbie says his behaviour is 'inappropriate' (p. 127), giving evidence that Marshall does not have the same social rules as the other people at the Tallis house.

6.

- The Tallis estate is a sprawling country house and garden that are richly decorated with 'Chippendale' furniture (p. 45), a lake, a library and an island temple.
- The class system in Part One is maintained with servants and gardeners being employed to work at the house, although Robbie Turner's involvement with the family suggests that these barriers are being broken down.
- During the war the park is 'ploughed up for corn' (p. 333) and the young men that might have worked at the house have left to fight abroad.
- At the end of the novel in the 1990s the house is a business concern as a hotel rather than a family home.
- The island temple and lake are now a golf course, reflecting the loss of the family's private income.

7.

- Mace and Nettle rely on Robbie to read the map for them as 'the compass points meant nothing to them' (p. 193) due to their urban upbringing. This means they defer to Robbie's decisions on their journey to Dunkirk.
- They 'depended on [his] French' (p. 195), which he has learnt as part of his privileged education.
- When Robbie tells them to do something, such as check their weapons, they '[do] as they [are] told' (p. 197).

8.

- 'Exhaustion made him vulnerable to the thoughts he wanted least' (p. 202). Robbie feels the mental pain of dealing with the horrors of war as keenly as the physical 'precise and tight' pain (p. 202) of his wound.
- Robbie sees the particular horror of the image as a memory worthy of sharing in conversation with the French men as 'his own single, haunting detail' (p. 199), but he is so traumatised that he cannot bring himself to speak about it.
- Robbie sees Mace and Nettle's reaction to the limb as **symbolic** of the dehumanising effect of the war; it has become 'something that ordinary men could ignore' (p. 202).

9.

- Shakespeare's *Twelfth Night* is referred to by Robbie on two occasions – he played Malvolio in a production and he writes letters to Cecilia about it (p. 204). This is a play about misunderstandings (including a letter that is misinterpreted) and unrequited love, and so reflects the themes of *Atonement*.
- In prison Robbie compares his situation to that of the classical figure of Prometheus, who is punished by the gods for stealing fire by having his 'liver devoured daily' (p. 204). This reflects the theme of prolonged and terrible punishment that is grossly disproportionate and unfair, such as the one the innocent Robbie undergoes.
- Briony compares the elderly Lola to 'Cruella de Vil' (p. 358), which is a reference to the villainous character from Dodie Smith's *One Hundred and One Dalmations* (1956), reflecting Lola's 'lurid' and strangely sinister appearance.

10.

- The retreat in France leads many to believe that the hospital is preparing for a German invasion, and Briony feels a 'muted dread' (p. 284) at the idea.
- Briony is frightened that London will be flooded with 'poisonous gas' (p. 288).
- She also fears that 'German parachutists' will spread out across London (p. 318).

11.

- Like Robbie, Briony's education and knowledge of French puts her in a situation where she can be of great help in a war situation and it is implied that the whole conversation takes place in French, demonstrating Briony's considerable capabilities.
- Briony is torn between her professional training and her compassion for the boy – she 'hesitate[s]' to tell him her name (p. 306) as that is against the rules, but she does so anyway, her humanity winning out.
- However, Briony's inexperience as a nurse is depicted as she needlessly unbandages his head, revealing his horrific wound, causing her to regret her 'foolish' (p. 308) action.

12.

- Most significant: Paul Marshall's Amo bar – this symbolises Marshall's exploitative view of the benefits of the Second World War, revealing his ruthless and inhumane nature (and we see Robbie sharing one on page 239).
- Second in significance: the soldiers' meal on the farm in France, comprising wine and 'goose liver pâté' (p. 198), revealing the solidarity between the English and French men in the terror of the retreat to Dunkirk as well as unexpected kindness.
- Third in significance: Cecilia's abandoned meal, including egg powder and jam, which suggests she is 'soothing herself' (p. 339) in the face of Briony's unexpected and disturbing visit.

13.

- For: She loves her children and thinks about them constantly.
- For: She is abandoned by Jack Tallis who arranges his life so that he can be in London with his lover, which makes her a victim of his selfishness.
- Against: Emily arguably uses her migraines as an excuse to do as little as possible and withdraws herself from family life on many occasions.
- Against: Emily unfairly transfers all her resentment towards her sister Hermione onto Hermione's daughter, Lola. She accuses Lola of remaining 'guiltless while others destroyed themselves at her prompting' (p. 147). This is unfair and cruel.

14.

- At the start of the novel Danny Hardman, the son of one of the Tallises' servants, is sixteen. Unlike Robbie, he is not invited into the Tallis family 'inner circle' but he still gets drawn into events.
- He displays a fascination for Lola: Briony observes that he has to be told to stop staring at her when the Quinceys arrive at the house. His face shows 'tranquil incomprehension' and appears 'innocently cruel' (p. 48) to the young Briony.
- Cecilia and Robbie believe that it was Danny who raped Lola and they are devastated when Old Hardman dies, believing he was their 'only hope' (p. 335) of Robbie being proved innocent.
- We learn that Danny has joined the navy (p. 279) whereas the rest of the boys from the village have joined the army, which Cecilia, incorrectly, appears to take as further evidence of his suspicious nature.

15.

- Cecilia has to suffer the humiliation of her mother reading the private note from Robbie, which makes her feel 'unable to believe her association' with her mother and the rest of the family (p. 179). She is also forced to explain that she and Robbie were making love in the library.
- She is unable to visit Robbie in prison – it is implied that their sexual relationship would only 'inflame' him, so she is only able to communicate with him by letter.
- Cecilia cuts herself off from the rest of the family in her fury, accusing them of 'snobbery' and 'stupidity' (p. 209), and rejects her privileged upbringing to become a nurse, living in cheap rooms with Robbie.
- Briony tells us that Cecilia was killed in a bombing raid on London in 1940 (p. 370) – if she had not left her family, she may never have been in London at that moment, the reader might assume, and she may have lived a longer and more affluent life.

16.

- Luftwaffe (p. 214) = German airforce
- Jerry (p. 220) = British slang for German soldiers
- RAMC (p. 223) = Royal Army Medical Core
- tommies (p. 234) = slang for English soldiers
- BEF (p. 244) = British Expeditionary Force, i.e. the British army

17.

- The trainee nurses are all terrified of Sister Marjorie Drummond – McEwan describes her as swinging between a 'menacing meagre smile' (p. 270) or 'mirthless smile' (p. 271) and 'fury' (p. 270). Her aggressive manner is somehow intensified by its contrast with her 'motherly' (p. 271) appearance.
- Briony has endless petty rules to learn, such as folding blankets correctly and making sure bed castors are facing the same way (p. 270). These are intended as a 'stripping away of identity' (p. 275) of the student nurses so they become obedient.
- The nurses only have 'freezing water' (p. 272) in which to wash their hands.

18.

- The vase symbolises Uncle Clem's act of endurance and heroism in the First World War. The breaking of the vase by Cecilia could be seen to **foreshadow** the breaking of her relationship with her family.
- The final destruction of the vase by Betty the cook (p. 279) could be a result of the patchy mending by Cecilia. This could symbolise the end of the old Tallis family history.

19.

- Part One:
1. The play shows Briony's precociousness and ambition as a child wanting to be a writer.
2. The play is a focus for arguments and tension between Briony and the Quincey children, with Lola taking the main role being a particular cause for disagreement.
- 'London, 1999':
1. The play has been a uniting force for the next generation of the Tallis family and has been a way of celebrating Briony's birthday.
2. The line 'before we love, we must cogitate!' (p. 368) encapsulates the play's 'moral' or message. It particularly draws attention to the need to think carefully about how people should behave in their relationships. This could be seen as **ironic** in the light of Briony, Cecilia and Lola's experiences.

20.

1. The fountain plays a significant role: Cecilia's impetuous diving into the water to retrieve the vase is catastrophically misunderstood by the watching Briony.
2. Robbie recalls Briony's dangerous practical joke when she pretends to drown so that he will jump into a pond to save her (pp. 230–1). He wonders if this was symptomatic of an obsession with him, although Briony claims she only had a brief interest in him and then forgot all about it.
3. Robbie's acute need for water in France leads him to delirium and desperate actions.

··

Section Two: Working towards the exam
··

1.

- The grounds of the Tallis home as a landscaped environment – such as the 'artificial lake' (p. 19) – represent wealth.
- Cecilia's picking of the wild flowers for the guest room – in which Paul Marshall is to stay – begins the sequence of events that leads to Cecilia diving into the fountain after the broken vase.
- Briony's attack on the nettles gives the reader insight into her thoughts and emotions.
- Robbie ironically equates the 'magnificence' of the late autumn garden with 'the glorious momentum of his life' (p. 230), just before the incident in which Briony pretends to drown.
- The destruction of the French countryside is a key aspect of the war in France.
- McEwan uses a lexical field of flora throughout the novel, employing specific names such as 'elms', 'oaks' and 'rhododendrons' (p. 363), 'rugosa hedge' (p. 19) and 'Cedar of Lebanon' (p. 25), which may reflect Briony's attention to detail and research in the writing of the book.

2.

- The fact that 'Briony' as a character within the text itself has written the novel makes *Atonement* a work of 'metafiction'.
- The reader has to approach the text as a **postmodern** construction rather than a simple chronological **narrative**, with an ominiscient, yet unreliable, **narrator**.

- We have to question/re-evaluate whether Briony is capable of accurately depicting the thoughts that go through the minds of her mother, Cecilia and so on.
- McEwan is exploring the role of the writer – Briony herself says 'What are novelists for?' (p. 370), although the question is left open for the reader to consider.
- The reader may see the novel not just as a 'family drama' but as an apology and confession written by Briony for her family and the generations to come.
- Briony's invented different ending for Robbie and Cecilia leads the reader to question the veracity of her narration – Briony says her earlier drafts were 'pitiless' (p. 370) in comparison with this version.

3.
- Briony misinterprets the fountain scene and comments, 'What strange power did he have over her. Blackmail? Threats?' (p. 38). This also connects to the themes of appearance, reality and the limits of human perception.
- Briony's accusation of Robbie – she believes that he is a 'maniac' (p. 168) – is a misunderstanding that Lola also colludes in.
- Lola and Briony are psychologically immature and unable to fully understand the surrounding adults' behaviour.
- Briony comments that 'it wasn't only wickedness and scheming that made people unhappy, it was confusion and misunderstanding' (p. 40). Briony, Robbie and Cecilia all suffer more from the consequences of their misunderstanding than Lola appears to suffer from her rape.
- The death of the woman and her son in France is a result of their inability to understand Robbie and vice versa – 'The woman answered but he did not understand her' (p. 236) – and this has a devastating effect on Robbie.
- Briony can never be forgiven by Robbie, who reacts to her with rage in Part Three because he cannot ever fully understand her motivations and desire for atonement.

4.
- Emily Tallis represents a traditional view of the role of women that has been inculcated through her limited home education and time spent at a private school in Switzerland (p. 64).
- She regards Cecilia's time at Cambridge University as 'childish', an 'innocent lark' and only a pretence of 'social progress', and believes Cecilia needs only to find a husband and 'confront' motherhood (p. 65).
- Robbie's mother, Grace Turner, reflects the vulnerability of women in the first half of the twentieth century, through her reliance on the kindness of Jack Tallis after she is deserted by Ernest Turner.
- The Second World War forced women into new roles and much more independent lifestyles, as Cecilia and Briony both reflect in their training and work as nurses.
- Briony the novelist is influenced by the work of female novelist Virginia Woolf, who was a groundbreaking writer (p. 282). This **alludes** to the developing voice of the female writer in the twentieth century.
- McEwan describes the criticism Briony receives from a colonel, who accuses her of 'meddling' (p. 360) in a topic she does not understand – this shows sexist attitudes that are common in large, traditional institutions such as the army.

5.
- A macabre text is one that involves images of death and violence that are unusual and shocking. *Atonement* contains some such images, although perhaps not as many as some of McEwan's other novels do.
- The way Lola Quincey reveals her bruises 'up to [the] elbows'

(p. 141) at the dinner party **foreshadows** the subsequent rape, but is misinterpreted by the other adults.
- In Part Two, the leg in the tree, 'pale, smooth, small enough to be a child's' (p. 192), is a macabre image that haunts both the reader and Robbie.
- Other macabre images include the horses waiting to be shot, the motorcyclist whose 'bloodied legs dangled' (p. 240) and the attack on the RAF man on the beach at Dunkirk, in which the attackers aim to be 'creative' in their violence (p. 252).
- The injuries sustained by the soldiers on Briony's hospital ward are grotesque and macabre. Note McEwan's use of domestic and familiar images such as the suppurating wound that has the appearance of 'miniature bunches of red grapes' (p. 296).
- The most shocking image is Luc Cornet's 'missing portion of skull' (p. 308). This encounter conveys both Briony's inexperience (at agreeing to remove Luc's bandage) and her determined and compassionate nursing persona.

Part Three: Characters and themes

Section One: Check your understanding

1.
- Both sisters have experienced the neglectful and distant parenting of Emily and Jack Tallis.
- Both are characters on the edge of life transitions at the opening of the novel – Cecilia is a young woman on the verge of adulthood – Briony is making the transition from childhood to adolescence.
- Both sisters grow distant from the Tallis family and both train to be nurses, although Cecilia actively rejects her family whereas Briony's motivations come from remorse and a need for atonement.
- Briony learns empathy through experience, whereas Cecilia seems to regard empathy as a weakness.

2.
- Leon stands in contrast to his two sisters at the start of the novel; while they are tortured with self-doubt and self-consciousness, it is noted that Leon's 'equanimity was bottomless' (p. 108).
- Leon brings the sinister Paul Marshall, 'the chocolate millionaire' (p. 26), to the Tallis household, and invites Robbie to the evening meal.
- Leon ends the novel as a frail gentleman in a wheelchair. He has, however, had a long and adventurous life with four marriages, suggesting that 'blandness' (p. 108) is not necessarily a barrier to success.
- Leon often provides humour and shows the gentler sides of Cecilia and Briony.

3.
- Emily Tallis initially misinterprets Paul Marshall's behaviour with the children as being friendly and playful.
- Robbie falsely believes that Briony accused him of raping Lola because she had a childhood crush on him.
- Briony falsely believes that Robbie orders Cecilia to jump into the fountain.
- The major from the Buffs in France (p. 220) wrongly believes he can flush out a group of Germans from the woods with just a handful of men.

4.
- Leon unwittingly mortifies Cecilia when he asks, 'Have you

behaved even worse than usual today?' (p. 129) at the dinner party after she has made love to Robbie in the library.

- Briony misunderstands the nurse's name badge and questions why it says 'N. Tallis' (p. 275), resulting in humiliation.
- Grace Turner is humiliated by the arrest of Robbie at the end of Part Two.
- The elderly Briony is humiliated and embarrassed by her incorrect assumption that her West Indian taxi driver is poorly educated when in fact he is a lawyer.

5.
- The lonely and bewildered twins symbolise the impact of absent parents.
- The way Jackson is punished for wetting the bed portrays a different set of attitudes towards children in the 1930s.
- The twins' decision to run away develops the theme of the devastating consequences of single events, which is often found in McEwan's novels.
- The twins are mainly presented as children (by the end of the novel Jackson has died) and portray the theme of troubled and difficult childhoods.

6.
- Cecilia and Robbie have both studied English literature at Cambridge and are both steeped in classic works of literature at the start of the novel, having recently graduated.
- Robbie regularly reflects on poetry and plays he has read and identifies his relationship with Cecilia as having links with fictional characters, such as 'Venus and Adonis' (p. 204), contributing to the theme of love and its fictional presentation.
- Cecilia quotes from W. H. Auden in a letter to Robbie (p. 203), and even in their run-down flat in London Cecilia has books by Shakespeare, Crabbe and Housman on the shelf (p. 335), suggesting the nourishing and comforting presence of literature in the midst of anger and conflict.

7.
- We learn he is resilient and adaptable, having joined the army straight from prison.
- Turner is compassionate and sensitive – the sight of death and dismemberment traumatises him greatly.
- The natural respect he is given by Nettle and Mace suggests that, although he technically has a working-class background, his 'adoption' by the Tallises has given him confidence and natural leadership.
- Turner is physically tough and resilient – he reaches Dunkirk despite his blood poisoning (although it may be that he dies there).

8.
- The main type of love portrayed in *Atonement* is sexual, passionate love as shown by Cecilia and Robbie – this love overwhelms both characters and directs their future.
- Robbie's love for Cecilia sustains him through prison and wartime, despite the fact it has been built on minimal contact and intimacy.
- Briony's love for her sister results in her remorse at falsely accusing Robbie of rape, and drives her to become a nurse in emulation of Cecilia and to humiliate herself by desperately seeking Cecilia's forgiveness.
- The love between parents and children is problematic in *Atonement* – Emily Tallis genuinely loves her children but is idle and withdrawn from them. The Quincey parents have apparently abandoned their children altogether.
- Briony marries, but seeking atonement is a greater part of her life than seeking love.

9.
- Danny Hardman – unlike Robbie Turner – does not have the good fortune to be 'adopted' by the Tallis family.
- Briony suspects Danny of having an unhealthy interest in Lola – this foreshadows Lola's sexual assault later in the book, and for much of the book Cecilia and Robbie believe that Danny did indeed assault Lola.
- Grace Turner is a recipient of the Tallises' beneficence – Jack Tallis ensures she is not left homeless when her husband disappears.
- Grace Turner's vocal anger at Robbie's arrest stands in stark contrast to the Tallises' silent bewilderment.

10.
1. The young Briony sees her play as a 'self-contained world she had drawn with clear and perfect lines' (p. 36), which is why she resents the interference of actors.
2. Briony decides that writing stories is more satisfying than writing plays, observing that 'a story was a form of telepathy' (p. 37) through which she could directly communicate with her readers.
3. As a nurse, the adult Briony continues to write, believing it is 'the only place she could be free' (p. 280).

Section Two: Working towards the exam

1.
- Emily Tallis spends so much time shut away, she cannot be presented through dialogue and interaction – writing from her point of view gives McEwan a way of exploring her character.
- There are moments of dramatic **irony** when the **narrator** switches; for example, Emily mishears what is happening between Paul Marshall and Lola.
- The changes between voices in Part One is disorientating but can be seen as Briony's attempt at a **modernist** style.
- The chapters from Cecilia's point of view allow the reader to see the depth of Cecilia's love for Robbie – something she is not able to voice with the arrival of the police and Robbie's arrest.
- Robbie's experiences in France could be said to be directly caused by his arrest – if he had been able to train as a doctor, he would not have been sent to war as a private soldier. Briony's imaginative depiction of his terrible experiences is part of her atonement for that.
- It could be argued that, by taking on so many different points of view and voices, Briony is fully exploring the effect of her actions.

2.
- It is not a 'traditional' love story, but a love affair is at the centre of the **narrative**. As Briony says, 'There was a crime. But there were also the lovers' (p. 370).
- The reader is in no doubt about Robbie and Cecilia's enduring love for one another.
- The story is written as atonement for the destruction of that love.
- However, very few other real love affairs are described.
- Much more of the novel is about war and social class.
- The novel ends with Briony imagining Robbie and Cecilia 'still alive, still in love' (p. 372), which implies love is the most important theme.

3.
- Briony cannot publish her book because of the threat of litigation from the Marshalls, so she has not been able to atone publicly.

- However, she has devoted much of her life to Cecilia and Robbie and to trying to articulate the consequences of her behaviour fully.
- Briony suggests she is acting in 'kindness' by giving the lovers 'happiness', even if it is in her imagination (p. 372).
- Briony is shown as being loved and celebrated by her family in the final chapter, which is a 'pleasant surprise' (p. 364). This could suggest that she has achieved atonement to some extent.
- Briony describes herself as a child as 'that busy, priggish, conceited little girl' (p. 367); openly criticising herself and displaying her faults can be seen as part of her atonement.
- Briony refuses to allow herself to imagine that Robbie and Cecilia can 'forgive' her – her ongoing acknowledgment of her guilt is an important part of her atonement.

Part Four: Genre, structure and language

Section One: Check your understanding

1.
- For: The crime of rape against Lola forms the climax of Part One and is the most shocking and memorable element of the book.
- For: The book examines a range of crimes and criminal behaviour, such as Marshall's abuse of Lola, and also the crimes committed in France during the war, such as violence and theft.
- Against: Lola's rape has fewer consequences than the fact of Briony's false accusation. Paul Marshall's marriage to Lola appears outwardly to be a successful and compatible union, despite its horrific background.
- Against: There are many more themes in *Atonement* – much more of the book is dedicated to exploring the nature of love and family ties, for example.

2.
- Lola is fifteen years old and crosses and recrosses the boundary between being a child and an adult.
- Jackson and Pierrot are powerless and vulnerable as children. McEwan reminds us of the terrifying (if sometimes inadvertent) world of adults.
- Luc Cornet is barely into his adulthood but dies a terrible death as a result of his injuries.
- McEwan depicts children in France who are killed and maimed by the relentless military onslaught – the image of the child's leg in the tree being particularly traumatic.

3.
- The sections allow McEwan to examine the story from different points of view. For example, in Chapter One we can see inside the mind of a number of the main characters, which helps to set the scene.
- Placing the action in northern France in Part Two enables McEwan to switch to Robbie as **narrator**. This foregrounds Robbie's importance as a character, and allows the reader to understand more fully the devastating effect of his separation from Cecilia as a result of his imprisonment.
- Part Three enables the reader to see the war from Briony's point of view and to understand the fundamental effect her false accusation has had on her life and the atonement she is trying to make for it.
- 'London, 1999' allows McEwan to jump in time to the 'present' and to reveal the true narrator of the novel.

4.
- We have a different perspective of the friendly and fun Leon – Emily sees him instead as having 'diminishing' prospects, in contrast to his father (p. 64).
- We get an insight into a traditional upper-middle-class woman's concerns: the 'heat' (p. 64) and Emily's desperation for Cecilia to marry.
- Humour is created by Emily's total misreading of the family: she labels the Quincey children as 'hard-bitten' and 'wiry' (p. 65) when in fact the reader sees how vulnerable the children are.

5.
- 'smoke rising from the blacksmith's forge, and a cobbled road twisting away into the green shade' (p. 37): this takes images directly from a child's fairy tale.
- 'what she saw in the bilious mélange of green and orange was not shock' (p. 29): the words 'bilious' and 'mélange' are unusual and obscure for a child to use.
- 'The advance of Lola's dominion was merciless' (p. 15): an example of Briony's childish hyperbole.

6.
- The labyrinth is a man-made, artificial place in which a person easily finds themselves lost and potentially in danger.
- This is a suitable **metaphor** for Briony because she has caused herself to be in this situation, and the verb 'marched' further suggests that she has acted purposefully.
- The situation is also a labyrinth because of its complexity; there is a great deal of importance placed on Briony's accusation and so it becomes increasingly hard for her to take back what she has said.
- To admit she was wrong would also open her up to anger from Cecilia and Robbie, which is something the adult Briony has to finally confront – the child Briony is not able to do so.

7.
- Briony uses the word 'maniac' to describe Robbie, seeing it as a 'medical diagnosis' (p. 119). However, labelling Robbie like this appears to solidify Briony's idea that Robbie is somehow dangerous.
- Briony goes on to generalise about the threat Robbie poses, commenting, 'Maniacs can attack anyone' (p. 120).
- It is a terrible coincidence that Briony immediately walks in on Cecilia and Robbie in the library, and she misinterprets their love-making as a violent act.
- Robbie has catastrophically provided Briony with more evidence that he is, indeed, a 'maniac'.
- When Briony encounters Lola after the rape, she says 'It was Robbie, wasn't it?' (p. 166), but in her mind she is thinking 'The maniac.'

8.
- Leon has nicknames for the family such as 'Sis-Celia' (p. 47) and 'Cee' for Cecilia (p. 129) and 'The Old Man' (p. 128) for his father. This shows his affection for his sister, but hints at a lack of respect for the absentee Jack Tallis.
- Leon uses slang such as 'a bit rich' (p. 52) and 'I'm half stewed' (p. 106), which reflects the typical slang of the 1930s, and shows Leon's casual attitude towards politeness and formality.

9.
- The word 'extrinsic' is used here to describe the prince, suggesting that he comes from a distant place. However, it is a misuse of the word that more usually describes objects or ideas, not people, and it has a jarring effect here.
- The rhyming of 'Eastbourne' and 'first born' is bathetic, with the choice of Eastbourne as a destination for a runaway bride being oddly incongruous.

10.

- The flowers that Cecilia picks show Cecilia's lack of confidence about her external appearance and her concern to make things right. This leads to her trying to find 'natural' water for them from the fountain.
- The nettles that Briony slashes are, in Briony's mind, **symbolic** of Lola Quincey. This is Briony's honest depiction of her dislike of Lola.
- The temple in the garden was originally built as part of the Adam-style house that the current Tallis house replaced. It is symbolic of 'old wealth' against the Tallises' new upper middle class. Its decline is symptomatic of the changing social structures in the twentieth century.

Section Two: Working towards the exam

1.

- We learnt that Briony is the author of the book in Part Three, but this chapter explores further the implications of this now the book is complete.
- Briony's diagnosis of 'vascular dementia' (p. 354) could imply that her memories are not entirely reliable.
- We learn that she is unlikely to be able to publish the book in her lifetime, so it may be she has not had to be so strict about being truthful after all.
- Cecilia and Robbie's letters are archived in 'the War Museum' (p. 371), which gives a sense of realism.
- The history of the Tallis house and the Tallis family since the Second World War sometimes shows continuity. For instance, Leon has continued through his life to be a charming if unambitious man. However, the change of the status of the house itself to that of a hotel shows the unstoppable movement in social structure that appeared so fixed in Part One.
- We learn that Robbie and Cecilia died in the Second World War, which adds a tragic poignancy to Briony's continued efforts to achieve atonement – 'There is no one ... she can appeal to' (p. 371).

2.

- Part Two shocks the reader by placing the action right in the middle of the war in France: it is a huge jump in setting and chronology.
- The opening paragraph where Robbie appears confused about the whereabouts of the map that is 'still in his hand' (p. 191) creates tension.
- Robbie's intention 'simply ... to survive' (p. 191) only makes an elliptical reference to previous unpleasant events, creating tension through the lack of information.
- Robbie and the other soldiers seem almost permanently bewildered and semi-lost. The misunderstandings and desperation create tension.
- The section that describes the meeting with Robbie and Cecilia creates a disorientating contrast or **metanarrative**.
- McEwan also diverts the reader in the section where Robbie recalls the time when Briony pretends to drown so that he will save her (pp. 229–34).

3.

- The attention to historical detail regarding the architecture and objects in the Tallis house (the Chesterfield sofa and so on) adds realism.
- There are references to archives, retained letters and so on – these emphasise the importance of recorded fact.
- The historical details of the Second World War, both in London and in France, create the realism of the novel.
- There is a tension between 'fact' and imaginative recreation in the novel: the sections from the point of view of characters other than Briony's (the whole of Part Two, for example) are completely constructed by Briony the novelist – factual details help to convey veracity.
- For the purposes of a book, feelings and personal responses are paramount elements.
- The title *Atonement* refers to a mental journey rather than a physical feature or fact, maybe suggesting that this is more important than realism ultimately.

Part Five: Contexts and interpretations

Section One: Check your understanding

1.

- The retreat to Dunkirk reflects both Robbie's strength and doomed heroism in a military event that has similarly ambiguous outcomes.
- Uncle Clem's Meissen vase is said to have been made by the painter Horoldt who was a real historical figure – the vase is symbolic of the family's wealth and long history.
- CC is generally regarded to be Cyril Connolly (1903–74), who was the writer and editor of the *Horizon* literary journal and a novelist. He was very influential in shaping new styles of writing, and gives *Atonement* a sense of being a genuine work of literature.

2.

- Betty the cook: an important part of the upper-middle-class pre-war household, but her arguments with Emily Tallis over meals (p. 105) and with Jack Tallis over a lost ration book (p. 279) suggest a lack of traditional working-class deference.
- Danny Hardman: as the son of the Tallises' handyman he is suspected of unhealthy interest in and assaulting Lola – arguably because of his working-class demeanour and position.
- Nettle and Mace: as working-class soldiers, they appear to automatically respect Robbie Turner, whom they perceive to be of a higher social class than them, even though he is not in military command.

3.

- The Tallises own a Chippendale sofa (p. 45): this is an extremely valuable eighteenth-century item that demonstrates conspicuous wealth.
- The grounds contain a swimming pool and stable block (p. 49), which show the family's extensive leisure time.
- The grounds also contain an 'island temple' (p. 72). Although it is symbolic of wealth and tradition, its shabby condition, with parts 'rotting away' (p. 72), may **foreshadow** the changing nature of the Tallises' status.

4.

- For: Briony's taxi driver is a symbol of a new multicultural and democratic world: although he is fatherless (which in the 1940s was potentially a disaster for Robbie Turner), his mother is a doctor and he has qualified as a lawyer.
- For: Briony describes 'tourist London' (p. 356) – there would not have been tourists in the 1940s.
- Against: The Marshalls still have power and wealth.
- Against: The old traditions such as the Keeper of Documents at the Imperial War Museum are still alive.

5.

- The hospital provides a modern and organised environment with Sister Drummond's rules and regulations directing even the most mundane tasks.
- The meals are cheap and unpalatable, such as 'vegetables boiled with an Oxo cube' (p. 273), in contrast to the lavish meals at the Tallises' house.
- The privations 'close down Briony's mental horizons' (p. 275) and the minds of the nurses are described as 'vacated' (p. 276).
- This time in London is a rite of passage for Briony and allows her to slip the chains of her upper-middle-class background and to 'work for her independence' (p. 278).

6.

- Tallis house: spacious rooms; Cecilia used to live in 'chaos'; the staff are polite and friendly to Cecilia
- Life in London: 'confinement' (p. 335); now she lives a 'simple' life (p. 335); the landlady is rude and abrupt

7.

- The young Briony writes in a sensual and evocative style that could be described as **stream of consciousness** at times, such as in the description of herself slashing nettles (p. 74), where she concentrates on inner thoughts and the self.
- **Modernist** writers saw people being alienated by industrial processes and urbanisation – Briony is dehumanised during her nursing training, even to the point of not being allowed to tell patients her name.
- Modernist writers were more concerned with the human condition than with plot, and so the leisurely descriptions of Part One in particular are in a modernist style.

8.

- *Atonement* is supposedly a book that is written by a character in the book – Briony Tallis. This self-reflexive structure is a **postmodern** feature.
- Postmodern texts sometimes feature historically real people: the writer and editor CC (which the reader takes to be Cyril Connolly) comments on the structure and style of the text.
- *Atonement* contains alternative endings for Cecilia and Robbie.

9.

- The Tallis family have made their money through business and patents; they are not the gentry but are the bourgeoisie – a class that have gained power through money.
- Paul Marshall is able to financially profit from the war by selling his chocolate bars to the army. A **Marxist** reading may suggest this is financial exploitation of human suffering.
- The Tallis servants (the Hardmans, Betty the cook, the Turners) could be seen as the 'proletariat' – the workers that labour to support the bourgeois lifestyle, with little personal reward.
- The development of the Tallises' house into the Tilney Hotel could be seen as reflecting the way in which, since the 1990s, leisure activities have become capitalist ventures.

10.

- Emily Tallis is shown as having no expectations other than being a mother and wife; a **feminist** reading might suggest she has been restrained from independent thought and education by a male-dominated ideology.
- Emily's illness could be seen as a manifestation of her repression, just like the 'mad woman in the attic' in *Jane Eyre* – another wife who has been locked away by her husband.
- Emily does not question her role and assumes her daughters should live in a similar way. Briony and Cecilia have to make traumatic choices in order to gain their independence.

Section Two: Working towards the exam

1.

- The Tallis house is clearly wealthy, with the 'pool', the 'south garden' and the 'nursery' (pp. 9–10) – all features that signify an upper-middle-class lifestyle.
- The 'in-betweeness' of Robbie Turner derives from the 'enduring patronage' (p. 88) given to him by Jack Tallis, which funds him through Cambridge despite the fact that Robbie is the son of the cleaner.
- Danny Hardman is suspected of rape because of his low social class. When Robbie learns it wasn't him, he says 'we owe an apology to Able Seaman Hardman' (p. 347), giving him suitable respect.
- The landlady at Cecilia's working-class flat in wartime London calls Cecilia 'Lady Muck' (p. 334), showing Cecilia is now 'in between' class lifestyles.
- Emily Tallis's indolent lifestyle, typical of upper-middle-class women, has become an 'invalid's shadow land' (p. 103).
- The Second World War transcends class boundaries. The Tallis house becomes a hotel; through this, McEwan shows the changing class structures of England.
- However, the novel is not just about class – it is also about love, family, the search for atonement.

2.

- How 'great' is Robbie Turner? He sees studying English literature at Cambridge University as 'an absorbing parlour game' (p. 91), which shows his great intelligence, but has he done anything else to be seen as truly great?
- He appears to be at the height of his potential at the start of the novel – 'he was happy and therefore bound to succeed' (p. 90). This makes his 'fall' more shocking.
- Could writing the obscene note seem to be a 'misadventure'? It was written with love but not intended for Cecilia to see – it is an instrument of destruction for Robbie. This does not make a 'fatal flaw', however.
- Robbie is a brave and compassionate soldier who tries to save people from injury and distress, but there is little evidence that he is 'heroic'.
- An argument against Robbie's heroism is the way he is tempted to get involved with the attack on the RAF man and he puts himself in no more risk than the soldiers around him.
- Robbie's fall is caused by *Briony's* misadventure, arguably – he is not a tragic hero because of this.

3.

- The novel's free indirect voice presents the thoughts of Cecilia, Emily and Briony, all in different styles reflecting their personalities.
- The passages written from Cecilia and Emily's point of view are actually written by Briony, who is trying to explain and atone for her actions – is she a reliable **narrator**?
- The scene between the young Briony and Lola very much presents female voices as a signifier for vulnerability – Lola's voice is 'weak, submissive' (p. 165).
- Lola Quincey's voice appears silenced through her marriage to Paul Marshall – Briony describes her 'silence in the darkness' (p. 324) by the lake, but she is not presented as speaking freely through the rest of the novel.
- Sister Drummond has a distinctive and unsympathetic voice, in her bullying manner that depersonalises the trainee nurses: 'You are, and will remain, as you have been designated' (p. 275).
- Other women's voices are represented through Grace Turner, Cecilia's landlady and the women in France.

MARK SCHEME

Use this page to assess your answer to the **Practice task** provided on page 116.

Look at the elements listed for each Assessment Objective. Examiners will be looking to award the highest grades to the students who meet the majority of these criteria. If you can meet two to three elements from each AO, you are working at a good level, with some room for improvement to a higher level.*

> **'Plotting and calculation are central ingredients of crime literature.' Explore the significance of plotting and calculation as they are presented in two crime texts you have studied.**

A01	Articulate informed, personal and creative responses to literary texts, using associated concepts and terminology, and coherent, accurate written expression.	• You make a range of clear, relevant points about plotting and calculating across both texts, for example comparing McEwan with Shakespeare or Agatha Christie. • You use a range of literary terms correctly, e.g. **foreshadowing**, **metaphor**, **irony**, dialogue. • You address the topic clearly across both texts, outlining your thesis and providing a clear conclusion. • You signpost and link your ideas fluently about plotting and calculation both within and across the two texts. • You offer a personal interpretation which is insightful, well argued and convincing.
A02	Analyse ways in which meanings are shaped in literary texts.	• You explain the techniques and methods McEwan uses to present plotting and calculation through narrative viewpoint and revelation in plot structure. • You explain in detail how such examples shape meaning in both texts, for example the detailed but futile plotting that Hamlet undertakes that is presented by Shakespeare through soliloquies, in comparison to the free indirect voices presented by McEwan. • You comment on spoken language, setting and structure in a thoughtful, sustained way.
A03	Demonstrate understanding of the significance and influence of the contexts in which literary texts are written and received.	• You demonstrate your understanding of crime-writing tropes, presentations of victims and perpetrators, notions of guilt and innocence, agency, punishment and atonement. • Literary context: McEwan draws on the country-house novel and **postmodernist** texts such as the novels of Virginia Woolf in which inner voices and motivation or 'calculations' are often described in detail. • Historical or social contexts: part of the novel is set during the Second World War, and portrays the decline of the English upper middle classes. The gap in social class between Robbie and Briony arguably forms part of Briony's calculation behind accusing Robbie of rape.
A04	Explore connections across literary texts.	• You make relevant links between characters and ideas within a text, noting how Paul Marshall's unpunished crime and Robbie Turner's imprisonment interlink. • You make critical judgements about the approach to plotting and calculation in both texts, drawing comparisons and contrasts, for example commenting on narrative structure and McEwan's use of ambiguous and multiple narrative voices and how this challenges the crime narrative.
A05	Explore literary texts informed by different interpretations.	• Where appropriate, you incorporate and comment on critics' views of the extent to which the texts can be seen as crime fiction. • You assert your own independent view clearly.

* This mark scheme gives you a broad indication of attainment, but check the specific mark scheme for your paper/task to ensure you know what to focus on.